ACADEMIC
Listening
ENCOUNTERS

LIFE IN SOCIETY

ACADEMIC ENCOUNTERS

The *Academic Encounters* series uses authentic materials and a sustained content approach to teach students the academic skills they need to take college courses in English. There are two books in the series for each content focus: an *Academic Encounters* title and an *Academic Listening Encounters* title. As the series continues to grow, books at different levels and with different content area concentrations will be added. Please consult your catalog or contact your local sales representative for a current list of available titles.

Titles in the *Academic Encounters* series at publication:

Content Focus and Level	Components	*Academic Encounters*	*Academic Listening Encounters*
HUMAN BEHAVIOR High Intermediate to Low Advanced	Student's Book Teacher's Manual Class Audio Cassettes Class Audio CDs	ISBN 0 521 47658 5 ISBN 0 521 47660 7	ISBN 0 521 57821 3 ISBN 0 521 57820 5 ISBN 0 521 57819 1 ISBN 0 521 78357 7
LIFE IN SOCIETY Intermediate to High Intermediate	Student's Book Teacher's Manual Class Audio Cassettes Class Audio CDs	ISBN 0 521 66616 3 ISBN 0 521 66613 9	ISBN 0 521 75483 6 ISBN 0 521 75484 4 ISBN 0 521 75485 2 ISBN 0 521 75486 0

ACADEMIC Listening ENCOUNTERS

LIFE IN SOCIETY

Listening
Note Taking
Discussion

Kim Sanabria

Intermediate to High Intermediate

CAMBRIDGE
UNIVERSITY PRESS

PUBLISHED BY THE PRESS SYNDICATE OF THE UNIVERSITY OF CAMBRIDGE
The Pitt Building, Trumpington Street, Cambridge, United Kingdom

CAMBRIDGE UNIVERSITY PRESS
The Edinburgh Building, Cambridge CB2 2RU, UK
40 West 20th Street, New York, NY 10011-4211, USA
477 Williamstown Road, Port Melbourne, VIC 3207, Australia
Ruiz de Alarcón 13, 28014 Madrid, Spain
Dock House, The Waterfront, Cape Town 8001, South Africa

http://www.cambridge.org

The publisher has used its best endeavors to ensure
that the URLs for websites referred to in this book
are correct and active at the time of going to press.
However, the publisher has no responsibility for the websites
and can make no guarantee that a site will remain live
or that the content is or will remain appropriate.

First published 2004

Printed in Hong Kong, China
Typeset in New Aster and Frutiger

A catalog record for this book is available from the British Library

Library of Congress Cataloging-in-Publication Data
Sanabria, Kim
Academic listening encounters: life in society: student's book / Kim Sanabria
    p. cm. – (Academic encounters)
Includes bibliographical references and index.
ISBN 0-521-75483-6
    1. English language—Textboks for foreign speakers. 2. Listening—Problems,
exercises, etc. 3. Social problems—Problems, exercises, etc. 4. Readers—Social
problems. I. Sanabria, Kim II. Title. III. Series.

PE1128.B72475 2004
428.2'4—dc22

2004043558

Art direction and book design: Adventure House, NYC
Layout services: Page Designs International
Cover illustration: Private Collection/Diana Ong/Superstock

See credits on page 157, which is an extension of this copyright page.

Contents

Plan of the Book

Unit 1 Belonging to a Group
Chapter 1 Marriage, Family, and the Home

1 GETTING STARTED (pages 2–3)	**2 AMERICAN VOICES** (pages 4–8)	**3 IN YOUR OWN VOICE** (page 9)	**4 ACADEMIC LISTENING AND NOTE TAKING** (pages 10–16)
• Reading and Thinking About the Topic • Listening for Numerical Information	***BEFORE THE INTERVIEWS*** • Personalizing the Topic ***INTERVIEW WITH ROBERT:*** Growing up in an extended family • Listening for Details ***INTERVIEW WITH CARLOS:*** Growing up in a single-parent family • Paraphrasing What You Have Heard ***AFTER THE INTERVIEWS*** • Thinking Critically About the Topic	• Giving Oral Presentations *Students prepare oral presentations about topics related to their families and present them to the class.*	***BEFORE THE LECTURE*** • Personalizing the Topic • Note Taking: Listening for Main Ideas and Supporting Details ***LECTURE:*** Family Lessons (Ms. Beth Handman) ***Part One:*** Rewards and Punishments • Guessing Vocabulary from Context • Note Taking: Organizing Your Notes in Columns ***Part Two:*** Modeling • Guessing Vocabulary from Context • Note Taking: Organizing Your Notes in Columns ***AFTER THE LECTURE*** • Thinking Critically About the Topic • Sharing Your Opinion

Chapter 2 The Power of the Group

1 GETTING STARTED (pages 17–18)	**2 AMERICAN VOICES** (pages 19–22)	**3 IN YOUR OWN VOICE** (page 23)	**4 ACADEMIC LISTENING AND NOTE TAKING** (pages 24–30)
• Reading and Thinking About the Topic 🎧 • Listening for Specific Information	***BEFORE THE INTERVIEWS*** • Sharing Your Opinion • Personalizing the Topic ***INTERVIEW WITH HENRY:*** Living with teenagers 🎧 • Listening for Main Ideas ***INTERVIEW WITH VICTOR AND SAMIRA:*** The influence of peers 🎧 • Listening for Specific Information ***AFTER THE INTERVIEWS*** • Personalizing the Topic • Examining Graphic Material	• Conducting a Survey *Students conduct a short survey to find out what people think the most recent fads are. Then they share their findings with a small group or with the class.*	***BEFORE THE LECTURE*** • Building Background Knowledge on the Topic • Studying a Syllabus 🎧 • Note Taking: Listening for Organizational Phrases ***LECTURE:*** Culture Shock – Group Pressure In Action (Professor Iván Zatz) ***Part One:*** Reasons for Culture Shock • Guessing Vocabulary from Context 🎧 • Note Taking: Organizing Your Notes in Outline Form ***Part Two:*** Stages of Culture Shock • Guessing Vocabulary from Context 🎧 • Note Taking: Copying a Lecturer's Diagrams and Charts ***AFTER THE LECTURE*** • Sharing Your Opinion

Unit 2 Gender Roles

Chapter 3 Growing Up Male or Female

Chapter 4   Gender Issues Today

1 GETTING STARTED (pages 49–51)	**2** AMERICAN VOICES (pages 52–57)	**3** IN YOUR OWN VOICE (pages 58–59)	**4** ACADEMIC LISTENING AND NOTE TAKING (pages 60–64)
• Reading and Thinking About the Topic • Examining Graphic Material ☊ • Listening for Specific Information	***BEFORE THE INTERVIEWS*** • Building Background Knowledge on the Topic ***INTERVIEW WITH BELINDA:*** Gender discrimination in the workplace ☊ • Answering Multiple-Choice Questions ***INTERVIEW WITH FARNSWORTH:*** Gender inequality at home and in the workplace ☊ • Answering True/False Questions ***AFTER THE INTERVIEWS*** • Thinking Critically About the Topic • Examining Graphic Material	• Conducting an Interview *Students gather background information on problems that fathers who want to be active parents face today. Then they prepare interview questions on the topic, conduct interviews, and present their findings to the class.* • Giving Feedback on a Presenter's Style *Students take notes on the preparation, organization, and delivery of each presentation. Then they share their comments and constructive suggestions for improvement with the presenters.*	***BEFORE THE LECTURE*** • Building Background Knowledge on the Topic ☊ • Note Taking: Using Telegraphic Language ***LECTURE:*** Gender and Language (Professor Wendy Gavis) ***Part One:*** Gender-Specific And Gender-Neutral Language • Guessing Vocabulary from Context ☊ • Note Taking: Using Telegraphic Language ***Part Two:*** Questions and Answers • Guessing Vocabulary from Context ☊ • Note Taking: Using Telegraphic Language ***AFTER THE LECTURE*** • Applying what You Have Learned

Unit 3 Media and Society
Chapter 5 Mass Media Today

1 GETTING STARTED (pages 66–67)	**2 AMERICAN VOICES** (pages 68–72)	**3 IN YOUR OWN VOICE** (pages 73–74)	**4 ACADEMIC LISTENING AND NOTE TAKING** (pages 75–80)

• Reading and Thinking About the Topic
🎧 • Listening for Specific Information
	BEFORE THE INTERVIEWS
	  • Sharing Your Opinion
	
	INTERVIEW WITH CAROL: Problems with TV news
	🎧 • Answering Multiple-Choice Questions
	
	INTERVIEW WITH SHARI AND FRANK: Reading the newspapers
	🎧 • Listening for Specific Information
	
	AFTER THE INTERVIEWS
	  • Paraphrasing What You Have Heard
	  • Sharing Your Opinion
		• Giving Group Presentations
		
		Students discuss important events of the 20th Century. Then, in groups, they develop their own lists of important events and make presentations about them to the class.
			BEFORE THE LECTURE
			  • Personalizing the Topic
			  • Thinking Critically About the Topic
			🎧 • Note Taking: Listening for Signal Words
			
			LECTURE: From Event to Story – Making It to the News (Ms. Sarah Coleman)
			
			Part One: The Work of a Journalist
			  • Guessing Vocabulary from Context
			🎧 • Note Taking: Choosing a Format for Organizing Your Notes
			
			Part Two: Getting a Story into Print
			  • Guessing Vocabulary from Context
			🎧 • Note Taking: Choosing a Format for Organizing Your Notes
			
			AFTER THE LECTURE
			  • Applying What You Have Learned

Chapter 6   The Influence of the Media

1 GETTING STARTED
(pages 81–83)

- Reading and Thinking About the Topic
- Personalizing the Topic
- ⌒ • Recording Numerical Information

2 AMERICAN VOICES
(pages 84–88)

BEFORE THE INTERVIEWS
- Personalizing the Topic

INTERVIEW WITH EDDIE, LESLIE, AND RALPH: Opinions about media
- ⌒ • Listening for Specific Information

INTERVIEW WITH VANESSA, FELIX, AND RICHARD: Opinions about media
- ⌒ • Listening for Specific Information

AFTER THE INTERVIEWS
- Drawing Inferences
- Thinking Critically About the Topic

3 IN YOUR OWN VOICE
(pages 89–90)

- Conducting and Presenting Your Own Research

Students conduct "The Un-TV Experiment" and present their findings either to a small group or to the class. The experiment involves performing specific tasks that make viewers aware of how they are influenced by television.

4 ACADEMIC LISTENING AND NOTE TAKING
(pages 91–96)

BEFORE THE LECTURE
- Personalizing the Topic
- ⌒ • Note Taking: Organizing Your Notes as a Map

LECTURE: Dangers of the Mass Media
(Ms. Dedra Smith)

Part One: Issues of Violence, Passivity, and Addiction
- Guessing Vocabulary from Context
- ⌒ • Note Taking: Organizing Your Notes as a Map

Part Two: Issues of Advertising and Invasion of Privacy
- Guessing Vocabulary from Context
- ⌒ • Note Taking: Organizing Your Notes as a Map

AFTER THE LECTURE
- Applying What You Have Learned

Unit 4 Breaking the Rules
Chapter 7 Crime and Criminals

1 GETTING STARTED
(pages 98–100)

- Reading and Thinking About the Topic
- Sharing Your Opinion
- Brainstorming About the Topic
- ☊ Building Background Knowledge on the Topic: Technical Terms

2 AMERICAN VOICES
(pages 101–105)

BEFORE THE INTERVIEWS
- Examining Graphic Material

INTERVIEW WITH EVELINA AND ARPAD: Crime in society today
- ☊ Answering True/False Questions

INTERVIEW WITH GAIL AND TOM: Being the victim of a crime
- ☊ Retelling What You Have Heard

AFTER THE INTERVIEWS
- Examining Graphic Material
- Personalizing the Topic

3 IN YOUR OWN VOICE
(page 106)

- Sharing Your Opinion

Students use the board game "Find Someone Who . . ." as a tool for asking and answering questions about crime and criminals. They can respond with information they have learned earlier in the chapter or from their own knowledge. Answers count only if they are clear and well-developed.

4 ACADEMIC LISTENING AND NOTE TAKING
(pages 107–112)

BEFORE THE LECTURE
- Building Background Knowledge on the Topic: Technical Terms
- ☊ Note Taking: Clarifying Your Notes

LECTURE: Crime and Ways of Solving Crime (Professor Michael Anglin)

Part One: Types of Crime
- Guessing Vocabulary from Context
- ☊ Note Taking: Clarifying Your Notes

Part Two: Ways of Solving Crime
- Guessing Vocabulary from Context
- ☊ Note Taking: Using Your Notes to Answer Test Questions

AFTER THE LECTURE
- Applying What You Have Learned
- Thinking Critically About the Topic

Chapter 8 Controlling Crime

<table>
<tr>
<th>1 GETTING STARTED
(pages 113–115)</th>
<th>2 AMERICAN VOICES
(pages 116–119)</th>
<th>3 IN YOUR OWN VOICE
(page 120)</th>
<th>4 ACADEMIC LISTENING
AND NOTE TAKING
(pages 121–126)</th>
</tr>
<tr>
<td>

• Reading and Thinking About the Topic
🎧 • Listening for Opinions

</td>
<td>

BEFORE THE INTERVIEWS
• Sharing Your Opinion

INTERVIEW WITH DAVID: Preventing juvenile crime
🎧 • Listening for Specific Information

INTERVIEW WITH AMY: The prison experience
🎧 • Listening for Main Ideas

AFTER THE INTERVIEWS
• Paraphrasing What You Have Heard
• Examining Graphic Material

</td>
<td>

• Supporting Your Opinion
Students choose statements on the chapter topic with which they agree or disagree. They argue their opinions in small groups by using supporting information and transitional phrases that link their points. Then the class makes a master list of the supporting information gathered for each statement.

</td>
<td>

BEFORE THE LECTURE
• Examining Graphic Material
🎧 • Note Taking: Recording Numerical Information

LECTURE: The Death Penalty (Mr. Jonathan Stack)

Part One: Arguments Against the Death Penalty
• Guessing Vocabulary from Context
🎧 • Note Taking: Using Your Notes to Ask Questions and Make Comments

Part Two: Questions, Answers, and Comments
• Guessing Vocabulary from Context
🎧 • Note Taking: Using Your Notes to Ask Questions and Make Comments

AFTER THE LECTURE
• Summarizing What You Have Heard
• Thinking Critically About the Topic

</td>
</tr>
</table>

Chapter 10 Global Issues

1 GETTING STARTED (pages 140–142)	**2 AMERICAN VOICES** (pages 143–146)	**3 IN YOUR OWN VOICE** (pages 147–148)	**4 ACADEMIC LISTENING AND NOTE TAKING** (pages 149–155)
• Reading and Thinking About the Topic • Examining Graphic Material 🎧 • Personalizing the Topic	***BEFORE THE INTERVIEWS*** • Sharing Your Opinion ***INTERVIEW WITH BARBARA:*** Life in the city, country, and suburbs 🎧 • Retelling What You Have Heard ***INTERVIEW WITH KENNY:*** Pros and cons of city living 🎧 • Listening for Details ***AFTER THE INTERVIEWS*** • Drawing Inferences • Sharing Your Opinion	• Making a Questionnaire to Use in a Survey *Students work in groups to make a list of factors that can affect the quality of life in our living environment. Then partners use the list as the basis for developing their own questionnaires to find out what other people think are the most important factors.* • Conducting a Survey *Students conduct the survey they prepared in the previous task, analyze their data, and report their findings to the class.*	***BEFORE THE LECTURE*** • Building Background Knowledge on the Topic • Studying Handouts 🎧 • Note Taking: Using Handouts to Help You Take Notes ***LECTURE:*** Our Changing Cities (Professor Bryan Gilroy) ***Part One:*** Reasons People Move to Cities • Guessing Vocabulary from Context 🎧 • Note Taking: Combining the Skills ***Part Two:*** Changes in the City • Guessing Vocabulary from Context 🎧 • Note Taking: Combining the Skills ***AFTER THE LECTURE*** • Summarizing What You Have Heard • Giving Group Presentations

Author's Acknowledgments

Many individuals contributed to the production of this book. First and foremost, I would like to thank Bernard Seal, the series editor of *Academic Encounters,* whose vision and direction were constantly present. His sense of students' needs as they enter the world of academic discourse is exceptional. The person who worked most closely with me during the development of the final manuscript was Kathleen O'Reilly, who also deserves inexpressible thanks. Her creativity, patience, and respect are beyond what any author could hope to find.

Furthermore, I would like to express my gratitude to Jane Mairs for her deft and experienced supervision of the project, to Louisa Hellegers for guidance, to Anne Garrett, the project editor, to Mary Sandre for help with permissions, and to all the staff at Cambridge without whose "behind the scenes" efforts this book would never have come to fruition. Heartfelt thanks to Don Williams, the compositor, and Rich LePage, producer of the audio program, for their outstanding work.

Then, too, thanks to the people who form the centerpiece of the book: the interviewees and lecturers. You have been uniformly generous in providing me with hours of conversation and commentary, debating the various angles that might best capture students' interests. Speaking with you, and now reading your ideas, I am struck by what wonderful people I am privileged to know.

And to the students, faculty and administration at Eugenio María de Hostos Community College of the City University of New York, a special acknowledgement. No creative endeavor succeeds without a constant source of inspiration, and you have provided me with just such.

Carlos, Kelly, and Victor: what would I do without you?

Kim Sanabria

Introduction

To the Instructor

ABOUT THIS BOOK

Academic Listening Encounters: Life in Society is a content-based listening, note-taking, and discussion text. It focuses on topics covered in sociology courses offered in North American community colleges and universities. The student who will benefit most from this course will be at the intermediate to high-intermediate level. The topics included were chosen for their universal appeal, but as students progress through the book, they will also acquire a basic foundation in the concepts and vocabulary of sociology. The listening, note-taking, and discussion tasks through which students interface with the content are designed to help them develop the skills they need for study in any academic discipline.

The complete audio program for this book, which contains the recorded material for the listening and note-taking tasks, is available on both audio CDs and audio cassettes. An audio CD of the academic lectures, which are an important part of the audio program, is included in the back of each Student's Book to provide students with additional listening practice.

ABOUT THE ACADEMIC ENCOUNTERS SERIES

This content-based series is for non-native speakers of English preparing to study in English at the community college or university level and for native speakers of English who need to improve their academic skills for further study. The series consists of *Academic Encounters* books that help students improve their reading, study skills, and writing, and *Academic Listening Encounters* books that concentrate on listening, note-taking, and discussion skills. Each reading book corresponds in theme to a listening book, and each pair of theme-linked books focuses on an academic subject commonly taught in North American universities and community colleges. For example, *Academic Encounters: Life in Society* and *Academic Listening Encounters: Life in Society* both focus on sociology, and *Academic Encounters: Human Behavior* and *Academic Listening Encounters: Human Behavior* both focus on psychology and human communications. A reading book and a listening book with the same content focus may be used together to teach a complete four-skills course in English for Academic Purposes.

ACADEMIC LISTENING ENCOUNTERS
LISTENING, NOTE-TAKING, AND DISCUSSION BOOKS

The approach

Focusing on a particular academic discipline allows students to gain a sustained experience with one field and encounter concepts and terminology that overlap and grow more complex. It provides students with a realistic sense of studying a course in college. As language and concepts recur and as their skills develop, students begin to gain confidence until they feel that they have enough background in the content focus area to take a course in that subject in order to fulfill part of their general education requirements.

The format

Each book consists of five units on different aspects of the discipline. Units are divided into two chapters. Each chapter has four sections and includes an introductory listening exercise, a selection of informal interviews, an opportunity for students to conduct and present a topic-related project, and a two-part academic lecture. A variety of listening, note-taking, and discussion tasks accompany the listening material. Chapters are structured to maximize students' comprehension of the chapter topic. Vocabulary and ideas are recycled through the four sections of each chapter, and recur in later chapters, as students move from listening to discussion, and from informal to academic discourse.

A chapter-by-chapter Plan of the Book appears in the front of the book and an alphabetized Task Index is at the back of the book.

The audio program

The heart of *Academic Listening Encounters: Life in Society* is its authentic listening material. The audio program for each chapter includes a warm-up listening exercise designed to introduce the topic, informal interviews that explore a particular aspect of the chapter topic, and a two-part academic lecture on another aspect of the topic. Each of these three types of listening experience exposes students to a different style of discourse, while recycling vocabulary and concepts.

Tasks that involve listening to the audio material (for example, *Listening for Specific Information, Listening for Opinions,* or *Note Taking: Listening for Organizational Phrases*) have an earphones icon 🎧 next to the title. This symbol indicates that there is material in the audio program related to the task. A second symbol ▶ PLAY indicates the exact point within the task when the audio material should be played.

The complete audio program is available on both audio CDs and audio cassettes. An audio CD of the academic lectures is included in the back of each Student's Book to provide students with additional listening practice.

The skills

The three main skills developed in *Academic Listening Encounters* books are listening, note taking, and discussion. Listening is a critical area because unlike text on a page, spoken words are difficult to review. In addition to the content and vocabulary of what they hear, students are challenged by different accents, speeds of delivery, and other features of oral discourse. Tasks in the *Academic Listening Encounters* books guide students in techniques for improving their listening comprehension. These tasks also develop note-taking skills in a structured format that teaches students to write down what they hear in ways that will make it easier to retrieve the information. After the listening and note-taking practice comes an invitation to discuss. Students discuss what they have heard, voice their opinions, compare their experiences, and articulate and exchange viewpoints with other class members, thus making the material their own. Additionally, each chapter gives students the opportunity to work on a project related to the topic, such as conducting a survey or undertaking research, and teaches them the skills necessary to present their findings.

Task commentary boxes

Whenever a task type occurs for the first time in the book, it is headed by a colored commentary box that explains what skill is being practiced and why it is important. When the task occurs again later in the book, it may be accompanied by another commentary box, either as a reminder or to present new information about the skill. At the back of the book, there is an alphabetized index of all the tasks. Page references in boldface indicate tasks that are headed by commentary boxes.

Opportunities for student interaction

Many of the tasks in *Academic Listening Encounters* are divided into steps. Some of these steps are to be done by the student working alone, others by students in pairs or in small groups, and still others by the teacher with the whole class. To make the book as lively as possible, student interaction has been built into most activities. Thus, although the books focus on listening and note-taking skills, discussion is fundamental to each chapter. Students often work collaboratively and frequently compare answers in pairs or small groups.

Order of units

The units do not have to be taught in the order in which they appear in the book, although this order is recommended. To a certain extent, tasks do increase in complexity so that, for example, a note-taking task later in the book may draw upon information that has been included in an earlier unit. Teachers who want to use the material out of order may, however, consult the Plan of the Book at the front of the book or the Task Index at the back of the book to see what information has been presented in earlier units.

Course length

Each chapter of a Listening, Note-Taking, and Discussion book is divided into four sections and represents approximately 7–11 hours of classroom material. Thus, with a 90-minute daily class, a teacher could complete all ten chapters in a ten-week course. For use with a shorter course, a teacher could omit chapters or activities within chapters. The material could also be expanded with the use of guest speakers, debates, movies, and other authentic audio material (see the Teacher's Manual for specific suggestions).

CHAPTER FORMAT

1 Getting Started (approximately 1 hour of class time)

This section contains a short reading task and a listening task. The reading is designed to activate students' prior knowledge about the topic, provide them with general concepts and vocabulary, and stimulate their interest. Comprehension and discussion questions elicit their engagement in the topic.

The listening task in this section is determined by the chapter content and involves one of a variety of responses. The task may require students to complete a chart, do a matching exercise, or listen for specific information. The task provides skill-building practice and also gives students listening warm-up on the chapter topic.

2 American Voices (approximately 2–3½ hours of class time)

This section contains informal audio interviews on issues related to the chapter. It is divided into three subsections:

Before the Interviews (approximately ½ hour)

This subsection contains a prelistening task that calls on students to predict the content of the interview or share what they already know about the topic from their personal experience. Allow enough time with this task for all students to contribute. The more they invest in the topic at this point, the more they will get out of the interviews.

Interviews (approximately 1–2 hours)

In this subsection, students listen to interviews related to the topic of the chapter. Most of the interviewees are native speakers of English, but voices of immigrants to the United States also enrich the discussions. The interviewees are of different ages and ethnic and social backgrounds, allowing students to gain exposure to the rich and diverse reality of speakers of English. The interviews are divided into two parts to facilitate comprehension: each part can include from one to three interviewees.

Each interview segment begins with a boxed vocabulary preview that glosses words and phrases the student may not know. The vocabulary is given in the context in which students will hear it. Reading this vocabulary aloud and exploring its meaning within the context will facilitate students' comprehension.

After each vocabulary preview, students are given the opportunity to scan the upcoming task. Then they listen to the interview and go on to complete the particular task, which might include listening for main ideas or details, drawing inferences, or taking notes on the material to retell what they have heard. This approach provides a framework for listening, teaches basic listening skills, and allows students to demonstrate their understanding of the interviews,

After the Interviews (approximately ½–1 hour)
In this subsection, students explore the topic more deeply through examining graphic material related to the content of the interviews, thinking critically about what they have heard, or sharing their perspective. Most of the tasks in this section are for pairs or small groups and allow for informal feedback from every student.

3 In Your Own Voice (approximately 1½–2½ hours of class time)

This section continues to build on the chapter topic and is designed to give students the opportunity to take creative control of the topic at hand. Specific tasks, a brief description of which are provided in the Plan of the Book, are determined by the chapter content. They may include:

- *Personalizing the content,* in which students talk with partners or in small groups, sharing their experiences and supporting their points of view.
- *Gathering data,* in which students conduct surveys or interviews of classmates or people outside the class, or in which they undertake small research projects.
- *Presenting data,* in which students organize their data and present it individually or in small groups.

4 Academic Listening and Note Taking (approximately 2½–4 hours of class time)

This section contains a formal, taped, academic lecture related to the topic of the chapter. It is divided into three subsections:

Before the Lecture (1–1½ hours)
The first task of this subsection asks students to predict the content of the lecture, explore what they already know about the topic, or build their background knowledge and vocabulary by doing a task related to a brief reading, syllabus, or other written entry. As with Before the Interview, this section promotes the student's investment in the topic.
Each chapter then proceeds to an academic note-taking skill, determined by the language of the lecture itself and sequenced to build upon skills studied in previous chapters. The skill is explained in a task commentary box, and the listening task is designed to practice it. The recorded material used for the task is drawn from the lecture.

Lecture (1–1½ hours)
In this subsection, students hear the lecture itself. To facilitate comprehension, all lectures are divided into two parts.
Each lecture part begins with a matching or multiple-choice vocabulary task to prepare students for the language they will encounter in the lecture and help them develop their ability to guess meaning from context. Potentially unfamiliar words and phrases are

given in the context in which they will be used in the lecture. Reading the items aloud, studying their pronunciation, and exploring their use and meaning will prepare students for hearing them in the lecture.

Following the vocabulary task, students preview a comprehension task designed to provide a framework for their listening and note taking. The task may involve completing a summary or outline or answering comprehension questions. The task may recycle the note-taking skill taught before the lecture or add a related skill. Students are instructed to take notes during each part of the lecture, and then use their notes to complete the lecture comprehension task. Previewing the task will enable students to answer the questions in a more confident and focused manner.

After the Lecture (½–1 hour)

This subsection invites students to share their perspective through discussion questions that allow them to analyze the chapter content more critically. It may also present additional information or ask students to apply what they have learned.

GENERAL TEACHING GUIDELINES

1. Replay recorded excerpts as many times as you think will benefit the majority of students.
2. Encourage students to gain additional listening practice by listening to the chapter lectures that are on the audio CD in the back of the Student's Book. Depending on the level of the class, you may want students to listen either before or after you have played the lecture for them in class.
3. Homework assignments can include thinking and writing about discussion questions, doing Internet research, and preparing and rehearsing presentations.
4. If possible, pair students from different cultural and linguistic backgrounds.
5. Depending on your students' level of interest and time constraints, you may want to pick and choose from the activities in After the Interview and After the Lecture. It is not necessary to do all of them.
6. To some extent, the course material builds upon itself. Skills are recycled (see the Plan of the Book) and the level of exercises increases slightly in difficulty. However, it is not necessary to do the units in order, and you can skip ones that are less appropriate for your students.
7. If you prefer to read the script of a lecture rather than play the recording, try to match the natural pace of the recorded lectures.
8. Refer to the Teacher's Manual for teaching suggestions, answer keys, the listening script, and lecture quizzes and answers.

To the Student

Improving your language skills is a journey of discovery, allowing you to learn new things about other people and yourself. *Academic Listening Encounters: Life in Society* is like a compass or roadmap that can help you along this path. The material in this book is taken from the discipline of sociology: the study of people in society and the way we live in groups. You may find ideas that are new and also material that reminds you of your own community and personal experiences. Active involvement is at the heart of any type of learning, so you should use this book as a context for your own experience. The specific academic skills you can expect to improve are listening, note taking, and discussion.

Listening to people is often a challenge because they may speak quickly, use words that you have never heard, or interrupt each other. Lecturers do not usually speak in the same way as they write, and it can be hard to understand how a lecture is organized. This book will give you practice in listening to people of all ages, backgrounds, and regions, and you will gain confidence as your comprehension improves.

Secondly, the book emphasizes the tools that will allow you to become a better note taker. Note taking is a vital skill for all kinds of academic study, but taking notes on interviews or lectures is different from taking notes on text because usually you cannot go back and check your comprehension. Taking notes on recorded material that you can listen to again, however, allows you to do just that. You will learn how to use symbols and abbreviations that will help you take notes quickly, and you will also learn how to organize your notes in efficient ways that allow you to review the material easily. This will help you to develop the confidence you need when you are a participant in a conversation or at a lecture.

Finally, do not neglect the opportunity to discuss the material in the chapters. In this book, you may find ideas that surprise you, concepts that catch your attention, or stories that make you want to share a time in your own life with your classmates. Use the opportunity to develop your listening skills while you listen to others contribute their voices to the class discussion, Then take your turn at sharing your own impressions and experiences. If you are shy about speaking, consider that discussion is an art that we all continue to improve throughout our lives, and remember always that other people will be enriched by what you have to say.

Good luck with your academic studies in English!

Kim Sanabria

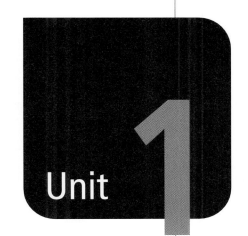

Unit 1

Belonging to a Group

In this unit you will hear people discuss what it means for an individual to be part of a group. Chapter 1 focuses on our first and most intimate group – the family. You will hear interviews about different kinds of families and a lecture about the ways that families teach children how to behave. In Chapter 2, you will consider some of the ways in which individuals are influenced by groups outside the family. You will hear interviews about peer pressure and a lecture on culture shock.

Marriage, Family, and the Home

1 GETTING STARTED

In this section you are going to discuss what it means to be part of a family. You will also hear information about the contemporary American family.

READING AND THINKING ABOUT THE TOPIC

If you read or think about a topic before you hear it discussed, you will find the discussion much easier to understand.

1 | Read the following passage.

What exactly is a family? The traditional idea of a *nuclear family*, meaning two married adults who live together and take care of their children, is becoming less and less common in the industrialized world. In the United States, for example, only about one quarter of all families have this structure. In fact, there have been such far-reaching social changes over the past century that the word family is becoming hard to define.

The concept of family has to take into account such social changes as industrialization, increased geographical mobility, and women's progress toward gaining equal rights. Other considerations include increases in single-parent families, cohabitation (people living together without getting married), divorced couples who marry other people, and other increasingly accepted alternative family structures.

2 | Answer the following questions according to the information in the passage.
 1 What is meant by a "traditional nuclear family"?
 2 Why is the word *family* hard to define today?
 3 What changes have affected family structure over the past century?

3 | Read these questions and share your answers with a partner.
 1 Has your own family been affected by the social changes mentioned in the passage? If so, how?
 2 How would you define the word *family* today?

♩ LISTENING FOR NUMERICAL INFORMATION

Listening for numerical information is an important skill to practice because conversations, interviews, and lectures often include this type of information.

1 | Before you listen to some information about trends in the American family, read the following questions and answers about current trends in family structure. Do you think the answers are true or false? For each answer, circle either *T* (true) or *F* (false). Compare your predictions with a partner.

Questions	Answers	Your predictions	
1 How many marriages in the United States end in divorce?	25% of marriages in the United States end in divorce.	T	F
2 How many children spend time in single-parent families?	About 50% of all children spend time in a single-parent home.	T	F
3 How big are average families in the United States?	There are about four people in the average American family.	T	F
4 What percentage of people live together before they get married?	About 50% of young couples live together before getting married.	T	F
5 How many people live alone?	About one in four households consists of only one person.	T	F

2 | Now listen to the information about trends in the family and check whether your predictions were correct. Cross out any false information in the "Answers" column and write in the correct information. Compare your answers with your partner. ▶ **PLAY**

2 AMERICAN VOICES: Robert and Carlos

In this section you will hear Robert talk about growing up in an extended family. Then you will hear Carlos discuss how he was raised in a single-parent home.

BEFORE THE INTERVIEWS

PERSONALIZING THE TOPIC

> Thinking about your own experiences and ideas related to a topic can help you understand and remember the information that you hear.

1 Work with a partner and compare your family backgrounds. Use the chart below each question to make notes about your and your partner's answers.

1 How many people were there in your household when you were a child? Who were they?

You	Your partner

2 In what ways was your family typical of other families in your community? In what ways was it different?

You	Your partner

3 What important lessons did you learn from your family? Can you describe one? For example, did anyone in your family ever explain to you why it was necessary to act a certain way?

You	Your partner

2 Work with a different partner and compare the information you wrote down in your charts.

INTERVIEW WITH ROBERT: *Growing up in an extended family*

Here are some words and phrases from the interview with Robert printed in **bold** and given in the context in which you will hear them. They are followed by definitions.

Probably the most important **influence** in my life was my family: *something that makes a strong impression on you*

not just my mother and father, but my **extended family**: *a family that includes many relatives such as cousins, aunts, uncles, grandparents, and several generations*

I grew up **very close to** my family: *closely connected by love for each other and time spent together*

I never really **sought** people **out** besides my family: *looked for*

My grandfather **wasn't retired**: *was still working*

He was more **protective** of us than my mother was: *watched over us closely*

some of my best **traits**: *characteristics*

Families are not necessarily **blood relations**: *genetically related; related by blood*

∩ LISTENING FOR DETAILS

Listening for details is an important skill to practice because it will help you improve your listening comprehension. To do this close listening, you have to concentrate and try not to miss any part of what a speaker is saying.

1 | Look at this representation of part of Robert's family tree and then read the questions that follow it.

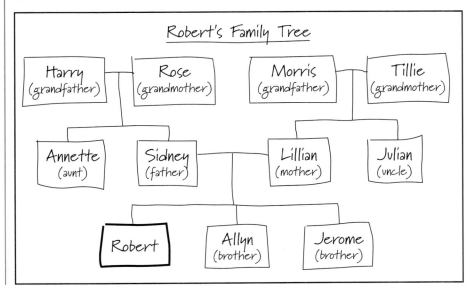

Robert's Family Tree

Harry (grandfather) — Rose (grandmother)   Morris (grandfather) — Tillie (grandmother)

Annette (aunt)   Sidney (father)   Lillian (mother)   Julian (uncle)

Robert   Allyn (brother)   Jerome (brother)

Robert

1 Where did Robert's parents and grandparents live?
   a in the same house   **b** in the same neighborhood

2 What kind of family did Robert grow up in?
   a a nuclear family   **b** an extended family

3 What was Robert's father's attitude toward him?
   a He was very protective.   **b** He encouraged him to live his own life.

4 When did Robert have a problem with his family?
   a when he was in his early teens   **b** when he went to college

5 How important were the other children in the neighborhood to Robert?
   a extremely important   **b** not very important

6 Where did Robert and his cousins often play?
   a on the block where they lived   **b** in the basement of their house

7 How did Robert's parents feel about his grandparents' values?
   a They rebelled against them.   **b** They shared them.

8 How much does Robert feel that families today have changed?
   a He thinks they have changed a lot.   **b** He does not think they have changed very much.

9 What does Robert believe is the most important characteristic of a family?
   a the fact that people are blood relatives   **b** the fact that people love each other

2 | Now listen to the interview with Robert and circle the correct answer to each question. ▶ **PLAY**

3 | Compare your answers with a partner.

INTERVIEW WITH CARLOS: Growing up in a single-parent family

Here are some words and phrases from the interview with Carlos printed in **bold** and given in the context in which you will hear them. They are followed by definitions.

That industry is **seasonal**: *the amount of work varies from one season to the next*

There was a **good stretch** when I was in junior high school: *a long period of time*

We'd just play **stickball**, and **marbles**, and **yo-yos**: *children's games*

I remember being taught to **pick up** after myself: *clean up, put things away*

I remember **running errands**: *being sent out to buy something*

It's important that you get **moral instruction**: *teaching about what is right and wrong*

an **anchor** in your life: *someone or something that keeps you focused on your goals*

School **was very influential** in my life: *had an important effect*

⌒ PARAPHRASING WHAT YOU HAVE HEARD

As a student, you will often need to paraphrase information that you have heard or read. That is, you will need to express the same ideas in your own words. When you paraphrase, you are showing that you understand and can remember what you heard or read.

1 | Read the following paraphrase before you listen to the interview with Carlos. Think about what kind of information might belong in the blanks.

Carlos

Carlos grew up in a _____
household. His parents moved from Puerto Rico to the United
States when he was _____, but his mother left
his father shortly afterwards. His mother was a garment worker,
and garment work is _____. Sometimes she
needed to work a lot and left the children alone. When Carlos was
older, he used to _____ with _____
_____ after school until his mother got
home from work.

    Carlos' mother taught him two important lessons about life: to
take _____ and to get
an education. As a child, he learned to _____,
_____, _____, and run
errands. He also studied _____ at home with
his mother.

    Carlos thinks that it is important for children to have someone
in the family who is a kind of _____ in their
lives. He thinks children are also influenced by people outside the
family. For example, he met a lot of good _____
when he was growing up who taught him many positive lessons.

2 | Now listen to the interview with Carlos. Try to listen for the information that you need to complete the paraphrase in step 1 and write it in the blanks. You may use more than one word in some blanks. ▶ **PLAY**

3 | Compare your paraphrase with a partner. They do not have to be exactly the same.

AFTER THE INTERVIEWS

THINKING CRITICALLY ABOUT THE TOPIC

You will not always agree with what you read or hear. Make it a habit to evaluate what other people say and compare it with your own knowledge and experiences.

1 Are the ways in which Robert and Carlos were raised similar to the ways you were raised, or are they different? Check (✔) the appropriate column. Then compare your answers with a partner.

Robert's and Carlos's Experiences	Your Experience	
	Similar	Different
Robert		
Grew up surrounded by his relatives	☐	☐
Lived close to his grandparents and other relatives	☐	☐
Was carefully protected by his parents	☐	☐
Spent a lot of time with his cousins	☐	☐
Carlos		
Spent a lot of time unsupervised	☐	☐
Was given a lot of independence	☐	☐
Was given chores to do and errands to run	☐	☐
Had a person who was a strong anchor in his life	☐	☐

2 Read the list in the left column. It shows changes that have taken place in the American family during the past century.

Changes in the American family	Positive consequences	Negative consequences
Divorce rates in the United States are higher than ever before.	Many people are able to escape from very unhappy relationships.	
People are spending much more time at work and less time at home.		Parents spend less time with their children.
Compared to a few decades ago, there are many more families where both parents work.	Men and women both have the opportunity to have a career and also have children.	

3 Work with a partner. Fill in the chart with as many positive and negative consequences of the changes in the family as you can think of. In your opinion, are these changes in the family harmful to society, or not?

3 IN YOUR OWN VOICE

In this section you will give an oral presentation about your own family.

GIVING ORAL PRESENTATIONS

In academic courses you will sometimes be called on to give oral presentations in class. Here are some guidelines to keep in mind:

- Plan what you want to say, but do not write it out and memorize it. Instead, make notes on index cards.
- Organize your notes carefully so that you present your ideas in a logical order.
- Using your notes, practice giving your presentation in front of a mirror or with a friend.
- When you give your presentation in class, speak slowly and clearly, and look at your audience.
- Consider using a visual aid, such as a chart, a map, photographs, or drawings, to help bring your presentation alive.

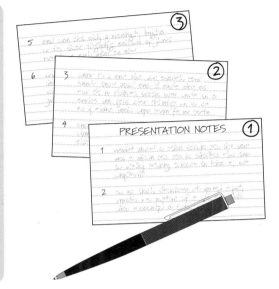

1 Choose one of the following topics about your family that you think will be of interest to your classmates.

   1 A family member who is – or was – an important influence on you

   2 An important lesson that you learned from someone in your family

   3 An object that has special meaning for your family (for example: a house, a photograph, or a piece of jewelry)

   4 A topic of your own

2 Plan your presentation carefully and prepare to speak for three to four minutes. Include the following information in your talk:

- the name(s) of the family member(s) you are speaking about
- one or two specific examples that illustrate the topic (such as an event in which something a family member did influenced you or the reason an object is important to your family)

3 Try to include a visual aid in your presentation. You might want to show an object, a photograph, or a map. If you do not have any of these items, consider making a poster that shows your family tree. Or you could make a drawing to illustrate your topic.

4 First, practice your presentation with a partner. Then give your presentation in front of the class. Be prepared to answer questions from your partner and your classmates.

4 ACADEMIC LISTENING AND NOTE TAKING: Family Lessons

In this section you will hear and take notes on a two-part lecture given by Ms. Beth Handman, an educational consultant. The title of the lecture is *Family Lessons*. Ms. Handman will explain how children learn lessons within a family, no matter what type of family they come from.

BEFORE THE LECTURE

PERSONALIZING THE TOPIC

1 | Work with a partner. Read the following eight examples of bad behavior in children listed below. Discuss the best and worst ways for parents to react to each of these behaviors. The "best way" means a way that is likely to teach good behavior to the child. The "worst way" is a way that will probably not be successful in teaching good behavior. Make brief notes about your ideas.

1 Sarah, a 2-year old, keeps throwing her food on the floor and cries until her parents pick it up.

Best way to react: _____

Worst way to react: _____

2 David, a 5-year old, is angry and frustrated. He hits his baby sister.

Best way to react: _____

Worst way to react: _____

3 Ronnie, a 6-year old, runs up and down the aisles when his parents take him to the supermarket and screams when they tell him to stop.

Best way to react: _____

Worst way to react: _____

4 Sheila, an 11-year old, is caught copying a classmate's test.

Best way to react: _____

Worst way to react: _____

5 Stephen, a 12-year old, takes money from his father's wallet.

Best way to react: _____

Worst way to react: _____

6 Tim, a 13-year-old, begins to smoke cigarettes.

Best way to react: _____

Worst way to react: _____

7 Erica, a 15-year old, refuses to go to bed until 2 A.M.

Best way to react: _____

Worst way to react: _____

8 Freddie, a 17-year old, comes home really late and won't explain to his parents where he has been.

Best way to react: _____

Worst way to react: _____

2 | Using your notes, compare your answers with other classmates.

🎧 NOTE TAKING: LISTENING FOR MAIN IDEAS AND SUPPORTING DETAILS

The first step in listening to a lecture and taking notes is to try to distinguish between the lecturer's main ideas and the supporting details. A supporting detail often consists of:

- an example, such as a story or anecdote
- an academic reference, such as a definition of a term, some statistics, the name of a researcher, or reference to a research study

Speakers may introduce supporting details with the following phrases:

For instance,	*X can be defined as . . .*
For example,	*According to a recent study, . . .*
Let me give you an example . . .	*It has been estimated that . . .*

1 | Listen to the recording. You will hear a few sentences from the lecture about each of the main ideas listed below. Try to distinguish the supporting details and decide whether they are examples or academic references. Put a check (✔) in the appropriate column. ▶ PLAY

Main Ideas	Supporting Details	
	Example	Academic reference
1 Children learn good behavior through rewards.	☐	☐
2 Another way children learn to behave is through punishments.	☐	☐
3 Parents can teach children by modeling appropriate behavior.	☐	☐
4 "Don't do as I do. Do as I tell you," doesn't usually work.	☐	☐
5 Parents worry about negative lessons.	☐	☐

2 | Compare your answers with a partner.

LECTURE, PART ONE: Rewards and Punishments

GUESSING VOCABULARY FROM CONTEXT

> When you hear or read words that you do not know, pay attention to the words in the surrounding context. The context can give you clues that will help you understand the new words. Using your knowledge of related words will also help you.

1 | The following items contain important vocabulary from Part One of the lecture. Work with a partner. Using the context and your knowledge of related words, take turns trying to guess the meanings of the words in **bold**.

_____ **1** I'd like to focus on three of the ways that children **acquire** their behavior.

_____ **2** A reward can be defined as a positive **reinforcement** for good behavior.

_____ **3** Most parents use rewards **unconsciously**.

_____ **4** Punishments are the second important way in which a child is **socialized**.

_____ **5** Both rewards and punishments are **controversial**. Many people think that they are not effective.

_____ **6** Some people argue that this reward is unnecessary because it is like a **bribe**.

_____ **7** The child should be taught that it's his **duty** to help with household chores.

_____ **8** Some of us grew up expecting to be **spanked** if we misbehaved.

_____ **9** Our parents may have hit us on the hand if we **talked back to** them.

_____ **10** Some children are subject to really serious **physical abuse**.

2 | Work with your partner. Match the vocabulary terms with their definitions by writing the letter of each definition below in the blank next to the sentence containing the correct term in step 1. Check your answers in a dictionary if necessary.

    a hit by someone as a kind of punishment
    b things that people have different opinions about
    c taught how to behave with other people
    d very hard and extreme physical punishment
    e encouragement
    f learn, get
    g without thinking
    h spoke impolitely to, argued with
    i something offered to someone to make the person do something
    j responsibility

🎧 NOTE TAKING: ORGANIZING YOUR NOTES IN COLUMNS

It is critical that you organize your notes in a format that helps you understand and remember the content of a lecture. You do not always have time to do this while you are listening to the lecture. The notes you take during a lecture are rough notes. But good note takers revise their notes as soon as possible after a lecture. You revise by putting your notes in an appropriate format and making any changes necessary to clarify the information.

This book will show you several ways to organize your notes. It is important, however, that you experiment and find ways that work best for you. Organizing your notes in columns is one good way to clearly show the difference between main ideas and supporting details.

1 | Look at these notes on Part One of the lecture. Notice that the main ideas are in the left column and the supporting details are in the column on the right.

Ms. Beth Handman: Family Lessons
            Part One: Rewards and Punishments

        Main Ideas   Details

1 Type of family (traditional or
  nontraditional) is not as important as
  love and support at home.

2 Three ways children learn social
  behavior from their families: rewards,
  punishments, modeling

3 Children learn good behavior through   - _____
  rewards.   - _____

                                            - finish homework — then TV
                                            - _____

4 Another way children learn to behave   - _____
  is through punishments.   - _____
                                            - _____

5 Rewards and punishments are   - _____
  controversial.   - _____

                                            - if parents are violent, children may
                                              become violent

2 | Now listen to Part One of the lecture. Take notes on your own paper. ▶ PLAY

3 | Use your notes to fill in the missing details in the column on the right in step 1.

4 | Compare the notes you took on your own paper and your completed notes for step 1 with a partner.

LECTURE, PART TWO: Modeling

GUESSING VOCABULARY FROM CONTEXT

1 | The following items contain important vocabulary from Part Two of the lecture. Work with a partner. Using the context and your knowledge of related words, take turns trying to guess the meanings of the words in bold.

_____ **1** Children's first **role models** are their parents.

_____ **2** There is an old saying in English: "Don't do as I do. Do as I tell you."
. . . But this **advice** doesn't work most of the time.

_____ **3** If you smoke yourself, it is probably **ineffective** to tell a child not to smoke.

_____ **4** Many people do not even realize the **impact** that they can have on a child.

_____ **5** It is common for babysitters, relatives, and **child-care centers** to take care of children.

_____ **6** The most important thing for children is to grow up in an environment where there are fair rules that are clearly established and followed **consistently** by everyone.

2 | Work with your partner. Match the vocabulary terms with their definitions by writing the letter of each definition below in the blank next to the sentence containing the correct term in step 1. Check your answers in a dictionary if necessary.

    a influence
    b not going to work
    c in the same way all the time
    d opinion about what you should do
    e people who are an example for them to copy
    f places where professionals take care of young children

∩ NOTE TAKING: ORGANIZING YOUR NOTES IN COLUMNS

1 | Look at these notes on Part Two of the lecture. Notice that the first main idea is number 6 because the last main idea in Part One was number 5.

Ms. Beth Handman: Family Lessons
                        Part Two: Modeling

          Main Ideas   Details

6 Modeling means: _____
   _____.

7 _____   · _____

8 "Don't do as I do, _____"   · _____
   doesn't work.   · _____

9 Modeling is the most important   · Children have many models:
   way children learn.   _____, _____,
                                            babysitters, professionals in child-care
                                            centers, each other, TV

10 Parents worry about negative lessons   · _____
                                           · _____

11 Most important thing: _____
   _____
   _____

---

2 | Now listen to Part Two of the lecture. Take notes on your own paper. ▶ **PLAY**

3 | Use your notes to fill in the missing main ideas and details in the columns in step 1.

4 | Compare the notes you took on your own paper and your completed notes for step 1 with a partner.

AFTER THE LECTURE

THINKING CRITICALLY ABOUT THE TOPIC

Work with a partner. Think of times in your own lives when your parents or caregivers rewarded you, punished you, or provided you with a clear model. Tell your partner about your experiences and compare your stories. Which of the three methods were successful? Which were not? Why?

SHARING YOUR OPINION

An issue becomes more interesting if you share your own opinion about it. Your ideas will probably be influenced by many factors, including your age, educational experience, and cultural background. It is likely that people with backgrounds different from yours will have different opinions.

1 Look at the pie chart and read the list of possible arrangements for preschool child care – ways that children who are not yet old enough to go to school can be cared for.

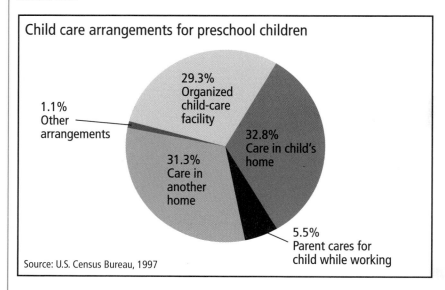

Child care arrangements for preschool children

29.3% Organized child-care facility

1.1% Other arrangements

32.8% Care in child's home

31.3% Care in another home

5.5% Parent cares for child while working

Source: U.S. Census Bureau, 1997

Possible arrangements for preschool child care:
1 The mother stays home and takes care of the child.
2 The father stays home and takes care of the child.
3 The child is cared for by a relative, such as an aunt, uncle, or grandparent.
4 The child goes to a child-care center.
5 The child has a babysitter at home.
6 The child is cared for by a babysitter in another home.

2 Review your notes on modeling from Part Two of the lecture. Then discuss the following question in a small group:

For each of the six possible arrangements listed in step 1, what are the advantages and disadvantages for children and their parents in relation to modeling?

You can use these phrases in your discussion:
- *I really think that . . .*
- *I strongly believe that . . .*
- *I am convinced that . . .*
- *I worry that . . .*

- *I am concerned about . . .*
- *The problem is that . . .*
- *The main advantage is that . . .*
- *A disadvantage might be that . . .*

The Power
of the Group

Chapter 2

1 GETTING STARTED

In this section you are going to discuss what groups you belong to and how groups influence behavior. You will also hear two college students discuss group pressure and you will compare their ideas with your own.

READING AND THINKING ABOUT THE TOPIC

1 | Read the following passage.

As individuals in society, each of us belongs to several different groups. For example, we are members of our own families, we have groups of friends, and we associate with groups at work and school. On a larger scale, we belong to a nation and maybe a religious group. Each of these groups has its own culture, or set of rules that governs the behavior of people in that group. For example, it is common for peers – that is, people of the same age or people in the same situation – to behave in similar ways or to share similar expectations. The groups we belong to influence our opinions about the world, our interactions with others, and the decisions we make. We may think that we behave as individuals, but in fact there are always group pressures that are influencing us to act in certain ways.

2 | Answer the following questions according to the information in the passage.

   1 List six groups that an individual can belong to.

   2 In what ways does belonging to a group influence our behavior?

3 | Read these questions and share your answers with a partner.

   1 Do you belong to any groups other than the ones mentioned in the passage? Explain.

   2 Can you think of a time when group pressure made you act in a certain way? Describe it to your partner.

⌒ LISTENING FOR SPECIFIC INFORMATION

As a student, you will often be asked to answer questions about specific information that you have heard. Preview the questions before you listen so that you know what information to listen for.

1 | Read the questions about "group pressure" situations below.

   1 You have been invited to the wedding of a family member you don't like. Everyone else in your family is going. Would you go to the wedding?

   2 Your friends are planning to see a popular movie this weekend and have asked you to go with them. You have read reviews that say it is a really bad movie. Would you go with your friends anyway?

   3 All your friends have started to wear a new style of shoes. When you first see the shoes, you think they look ugly. Would you consider buying them anyway?

   4 Your parents have been invited to their friend's house in the country for the weekend. They want you to go with them. You are in college and need to study. Would you go away with your parents for the weekend?

2 | Listen to two college students – Rebecca and Jim. What do they say they would do in these situations? Take notes about their answers. ▶ **PLAY**

Situation	Rebecca's response	Jim's response
1 Going to a relative's wedding		
2 Going to a movie		
3 Buying new shoes		
4 Going away for the weekend		

3 | Compare your answers in a small group. Discuss whether any of Rebecca's or Jim's reasons for their answers surprise you. What would you do in these situations?

2 AMERICAN VOICES: Henry, Victor, and Samira

In this section you will hear three Americans discuss one type of group pressure – *peer pressure* – among young people. You will hear Henry's perspective as the father of two boys. Then you will hear two young people, Victor and Samira, talk about the influence of their peers.

BEFORE THE INTERVIEWS

SHARING YOUR OPINION

1 Henry is an American father of two teenage boys. Read the behaviors in the chart. Decide which ones you think he would let his sons do.

	Would let them do it	Would not let them do it
1 Wear baggy pants	☐	☐
2 Dye their hair	☐	☐
3 Talk on the phone for a long time	☐	☐
4 Smoke cigarettes	☐	☐
5 Take drugs	☐	☐
6 Drink alcohol	☐	☐
7 Play video games	☐	☐

2 Victor is a young boy and Samira is a teenage girl. The interviewer asks them both this question:

> *Do you think your friends have a lot of influence on you?*

Which of the following answers do you think is Victor's (write *V*) and which do you think is Samira's (write *S*)? Why?

1 _____ "Well . . . sometimes."

2 _____ "Totally. I mean, we talk about everything, and, like, I have my own opinions about stuff and all that, but we always talk everything over."

3 Compare your answers to steps 1 and 2 with a partner.

PERSONALIZING THE TOPIC

Work in a small group. Make a chart like the one below. Fill in the chart with activities that your own parents or caregivers allowed or did not allow you to do. Discuss the reasons you were or were not allowed to do them.

Name of group member	Activities that were allowed	Activities that were not allowed

INTERVIEW WITH HENRY: Living with teenagers

Here are some words and phrases from the interview with Henry printed in **bold** and given in the context in which you will hear them. They are followed by definitions.

Adolescence is the time when the pressure begins to **shift**: *the time between childhood and adulthood / move or change*

comes into full bloom at about thirteen, fourteen: *becomes fully developed*

You can tell **at a glance**: *with a quick look*

with the hope that the **fad** would have passed: *a new fashion that is suddenly popular*

Where would you **draw the line**: *place a limit on what is permitted*

They can be talking **online**: *on the Internet*

Should you be trying to **monitor it**: *watch it carefully*

My kids **are into** video games: *have an important interest in*

🎧 LISTENING FOR MAIN IDEAS

Informal interviews and conversations are less organized than lectures or presentations. So, when you want to understand the main ideas, you have to think back over the whole interview or conversation and try to figure out what the people were trying to express.

Henry

1 | In this interview Henry gives advice about how to deal with teenage children. Before you listen, read the following advice that is commonly given to parents on this subject.

Advice to Parents on How to Deal with Teenage Children

_____ Be a good role model. Show them how to behave well by behaving well yourself.

_____ Let them make their own decisions about fashion when they are ready.

_____ Monitor their behavior.

_____ Give them freedom to experiment and have fun, as long as their behavior is safe and legal.

_____ Set clear limits. Be clear about what they can and cannot do.

_____ Listen to the way you talk to them. Try to avoid the annoying language that your own parents used with you.

2 | Now listen. Place a check (✔) next to the main ideas that Henry discusses from the list above. ▶ **PLAY**

3 Discuss the following questions with a partner.

  1 Do you agree with Henry's advice?

  2 Look back at your answers to step 1 of "Sharing Your Opinion," on page 19. Were your predictions about what Henry would let his sons do correct?

4 Another main idea that Henry talks about is the importance of peer groups. Read the two statements below and then discuss the questions that follow with a partner.

- As you get older, your friends become less important to you and your family becomes more important.
- As you get older, your family becomes less important to you and your friends become more important.

  1 Which statement expresses Henry's point of view?

  2 Which statement do you agree with more? Why?

INTERVIEW WITH VICTOR AND SAMIRA: The influence of peers

Here are some words and phrases from the interview with Victor and Samira printed in **bold** and given in the context in which you will hear them. They are followed by definitions.

Do you ever **change your mind**: *change your opinion*

She said it's **a waste of money**: *not worth the money*

I am just **jealous**: *unhappy and slightly angry because you want what someone else has*

loads of people: *a lot of*

the people you **hang out with**: *spend time with*

You can't **conform** all the time: *do what everyone else is doing*

You're **in the same boat**: *in the same situation*

Victor

Samira

🎧 LISTENING FOR SPECIFIC INFORMATION

1 Read the following questions before you listen to the interview with Victor and Samira.

  1 How old is Victor?

  2 Does Victor think he is influenced by his friends? Explain your answer.

  3 What does Victor want to get and why?

  4 How does Victor's mom feel about what he wants?

  5 What is Victor going to do about the situation?

  6 What grade is Samira in?

  7 Does Samira agree that her peers influence her a lot? Explain your answer.

  8 Who influences Samira more – her friends or her parents? Why?

2 | Now listen to the interview. Write short answers for the questions in step 1. ▶ **PLAY**

3 | Compare your answers with a partner and then with the class.

AFTER THE INTERVIEWS

PERSONALIZING THE TOPIC

Discuss the following questions with a partner and then share your ideas with the class.

When you were an adolescent . . .

1 Did your family try to influence the clothes you wore?
2 Did you ever have friends that your family did not like?
3 What time did you have to be back home in the evening?
4 Were you allowed to date?
5 Did you spend a lot of time alone?
6 Did your family have strict rules about what you couldn't do?

EXAMINING GRAPHIC MATERIAL

A lot of information that you find on a topic is presented in graphic form, so it is important to practice reading and analyzing graphs and charts.

One of the reasons that parents worry about adolescent peer pressure is that teenagers may start to experiment with alcohol, tobacco, and drugs. Look at the following chart and then discuss the questions below with the class.

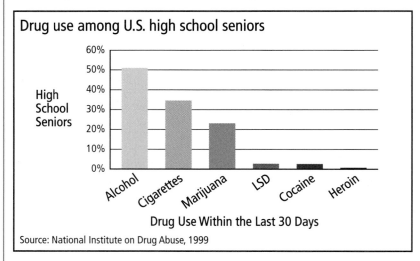

Drug use among U.S. high school seniors

High School Seniors

Drug Use Within the Last 30 Days

Source: National Institute on Drug Abuse, 1999

1 Describe the information in the chart. Does any of the data surprise you?
2 What do you think would be different in a chart about teenage drug abuse in your community?

3 IN YOUR OWN VOICE

In this section you will conduct a short survey to find out what other people think the most recent fads are. Then you will share your findings with a small group or the class.

CONDUCTING A SURVEY

When you are asked to talk about a topic to a group of people, it is often a good idea to collect ideas from your friends and other people that you know. Conducting your own survey may give you ideas that you had not thought of before.

1 | A *fad* is a kind of fashion that becomes popular very suddenly and then usually goes away suddenly, too. Interview three people outside your class about recent fads. Try to find people of different ages and backgrounds. Here is a way to start the interview:

> *Hi. I'm doing a survey for my English class about fads. Can you tell me about a fashion item that is particularly popular these days?*
>
> *And what about a food or drink item that is particularly popular at the moment?*

2 | Take notes on what the people you interview say. Write your notes in this chart. Also write down the age and sex of each person you interview.

Survey about Fads			
	Person 1	Person 2	Person 3
Age: Sex:			
Items That Are Particularly Popular at the Moment			
A fashion item:			
A food or drink:			
A game or sport:			
A musician or entertainer:			
A movie or TV show:			

3 | Now share your findings about recent fads with a small group or with the class.

**ACADEMIC LISTENING AND NOTE TAKING: Culture Shock –
Group Pressure in Action**

In this section you will hear and take notes on a two-part lecture given by Iván Zatz, a professor of social sciences and cross-cultural studies. The title of the lecture is *Culture Shock – Group Pressure in Action*. Professor Zatz will explain why and how culture shock occurs.

BEFORE THE LECTURE

BUILDING BACKGROUND KNOWLEDGE ON THE TOPIC

When you attend a lecture, you almost always know what the topic will be. It is a good idea to do some background reading on the topic first so that you can become familiar with some of the terms and ideas that are likely to be discussed by the lecturer.

1 | Before you hear the lecture on culture shock, it will be helpful to think about the concept of *culture*. Read the following passage about culture.

Culture has been defined as "everything humans are socialized to do, think, use, and make." In 1966, Edward Hall compared the nature of culture to an iceberg. You can see part of an iceberg, but most of the iceberg is below the water and cannot be seen. Similarly, most aspects of culture are not visible. These invisible aspects are things that we are familiar with but don't usually think about or question.

An example of an aspect of culture that is visible – one that is *above* the water level – would be the types of jobs that people have. In other words, the types of jobs may differ from culture to culture, and this is a subject that people commonly discuss. An example of an invisible cultural aspect – one that is *below* the water level – would be ways of being polite or impolite. Everyone in a society knows what behavior is polite or impolite, but they don't often think about it consciously or question it.

2 | Read the list of aspects of culture. For each aspect, decide if you think it would be above or below the water level of the cultural iceberg and write it on an appropriate line in the illustration on page 25.

- ways of showing emotion
- our ideas about what looks fashionable
- the ways older and younger people should behave
- the amount of physical distance we leave between ourselves and others when we have a conversation

- names of popular musicians
- our ideas about what looks beautiful
- the kind of food that is sold in supermarkets
- how late we can arrive at an appointment without being rude

ABOVE the water level: cultural aspects that are easy to identify and discuss
BELOW the water level: cultural aspects that are commonly understood but are not usually questioned

3 | Compare your ideas in a small group. Then, with your group, add other items that you think should go above and below the water level.

STUDYING A SYLLABUS

Many professors hand out a syllabus that includes a brief description of each of the lectures for the course. If you study the syllabus before a lecture and think about the possible content of the lecture you are going to hear, it will make the lecture easier to follow.

1 | Read the following description from Professor Zatz's syllabus.

Week 6: Culture Shock – Group Pressure in Action
– Definition of culture shock
– Reasons for culture shock
– Stages of culture shock
– Practical applications of research

2 | Work with a partner. Look up the definition of *culture shock* in a dictionary.

3 | Discuss the following questions with your partner.
   1 Why do you think people experience culture shock?
   2 How do you think people who have culture shock feel?
   3 Do you think that culture shock can be avoided? How?

4 | Compare your answers with the class.

⌒ NOTE TAKING: LISTENING FOR ORGANIZATIONAL PHRASES

Good lecturers make it easy to understand and take notes on their lectures by using organizational phrases. These phrases may appear in the introduction, the body of the lecture, or the conclusion. You need to listen carefully for these phrases because they will show you the way the lecture is organized and when the main ideas are going to be introduced. Here are some examples of typical phrases:

In the introduction	*Today, I'm going to talk about . . .* *First, I will . . .* *Then I'm going to . . .* *Finally, I will . . .*
In the body of the lecture	*So, first, let's look at . . .* *Now let's move on to my second topic, which is . . .* *Finally, I want you to consider . . .*
In the conclusion	*Let me summarize for you . . .* *So, the three main points that we have examined today are . . .*

1 The organizational phrases below are from the lecture. Work out the order in which you think they will appear. Write *1* next to the phrase that you think will come first in the lecture, *2* next to the second phrase, and so on.

_____ **a** Now let's turn to . . .

_____ **b** I'm going to focus on three main ideas in this lecture. . . .

_____ **c** Secondly, I will describe . . .

_____ **d** The subject of today's lecture is . . .

_____ **e** To conclude, let's look at . . .

_____ **f** First of all, we will consider . . .

_____ **g** Finally, I'll mention . . .

_____ **h** First, then, . . .

2 Compare your answers with a partner.

3 Now, listen to these phrases in the order that they actually appear in the lecture and note which comes first, second, third, and so on. Write the letter in the correct blank below. ▶ **PLAY**

1 ___ 2 ___ 3 ___ 4 ___ 5 ___ 6 ___ 7 ___ 8 ___

LECTURE, PART ONE: Reasons for Culture Shock

GUESSING VOCABULARY FROM CONTEXT

1 | The following items contain important vocabulary from Part One of the lecture. Work with a partner. Using the context and your knowledge of related words, take turns trying to guess the meanings of the words in **bold**.

_____ **1** Culture shock can be seen as **a manifestation** of group pressure in action.

_____ **2** Culture shock is **a complex phenomenon**.

_____ **3** Cross-cultural studies have **immense** practical value for modern society.

_____ **4** when you grow up in a particular **set of surroundings**

_____ **5** the rules and guidelines that **govern** the behavior of the people around you

_____ **6** The rules of a social group are not clearly **articulated**.

_____ **7** People often behave **irrationally** when they are experiencing culture shock.

_____ **8** It is a highly **stressful** experience.

2 | Work with your partner. Match the vocabulary terms with their definitions by writing the letter of each definition below in the blank next to the sentence or phrase containing the correct term in step 1. Check your answers in a dictionary if necessary.

a put into words
b not logically; not in a reasonable way
c something that is complicated and not easy to understand
d an example
e place; environment
f uncomfortable and difficult
g very large
h control

🎧 NOTE TAKING: ORGANIZING YOUR NOTES IN OUTLINE FORM

An outline is a traditional format for organizing notes in English-speaking countries. In a formal outline, main points are usually indicated as Roman numerals (_I, II, III,_ etc.). Under each main point there are usually supporting points – or details – that are indicated as capital letters (_A, B, C,_ etc.). Underneath these are Arabic numerals (_1, 2, 3,_ etc.).

Remember that you may not be able to organize your notes in the best way while you are listening to a lecture. But you should revise your notes as soon after the lecture as possible.

1 | Look at the outline of Part One of the lecture on page 28. Think about what kind of information you might need to complete the outline.

Professor Iván Zatz

Culture Shock — Group Pressure in Action

I Definition of culture shock = _____

II 3 Main ideas

    A _____

    B _____

    C Applications of culture-shock research

III Reasons for culture shock

    A one set of rules growing up — not often articulated

    B other countries — _____

    C can't use your own _____

        1 people act _____

        2 people feel _____

2 | Now listen to Part One of the lecture. Take notes on your own paper. ▶ **PLAY**

3 | Use your notes to complete the outline in step 1.

4 | Compare the notes you took on your own paper and your completed outline for step 1 with a partner.

LECTURE, PART TWO: Stages of Culture Shock

GUESSING VOCABULARY FROM CONTEXT

1 | The following items contain important vocabulary from Part Two of the lecture. Work with a partner. Using the context and your knowledge of related words, take turns trying to guess the meanings of the words in **bold**.

_____ **1** If you were to **depict** it on paper, you might draw a "wave" shape.

_____ **2** People do not usually react with fear. Surprisingly, there is often a feeling of **euphoria**.

_____ **3** You are **on your guard** because of the strangeness of the situation.

_____ **4** Differences are likely to seem exciting rather than **threatening**.

_____ **5** They might never **recapture** the honeymoon period.

_____ **6** Many societies have recent **immigrants**, sometimes in large numbers.

_____ **7** Cultural differences can lead to **tense** relationships.

_____ **8** tense relationships between different **ethnic** groups

_____ **9** Different cultures have to live in close **contact** with each other.

2 Work with your partner. Match the vocabulary terms with their definitions by writing the letter of each definition below in the blank next to the sentence or phrase containing the correct term in step 1. Check your answers in a dictionary if necessary.

  a watching for any danger
  b connection; association
  c get back
  d make a picture of
  e cultural or racial
  f stressful; not calm
  g dangerous
  h intense happiness
  i people who have left their country to live in another country

🎧 NOTE TAKING: COPYING A LECTURER'S DIAGRAMS AND CHARTS

Whenever a lecturer draws a diagram or puts a chart on the board during a lecture, you should always copy it into your notes. You can add extra information from the lecture to the diagram or chart as the lecturer speaks.

1 Look at the diagram that Professor Zatz put on the board during the second part of the lecture. This diagram represents the "wave" that shows the different stages of culture shock. Notice that the lecturer numbered the stages 1, 2, and 3.

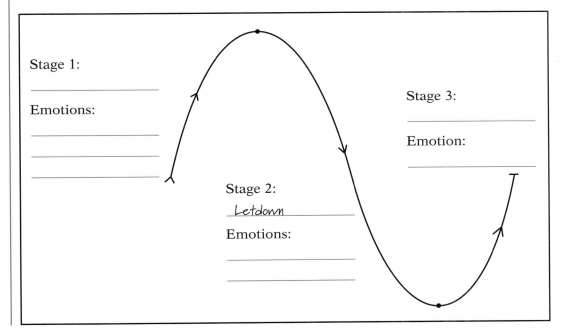

2 | As you listen to this part of the lecture, take notes on your own paper. Then use your notes to fill in the diagram with the names of the different stages of culture shock (in the left column) and the different emotions for each stage (in the right column). ▶ **PLAY**

Stages of culture shock

Letdown (becoming disappointed because something is not as good as you expected)

Honeymoon (feeling wonderful, like people who take a "honeymoon" trip after they get married)

Resignation (becoming accustomed to a new situation, even if it is difficult)

Emotions of culture shock

adjustment

loneliness

euphoria

excitement

confusion

enthusiasm

3 | Compare your diagram with a partner.

4 | Practice giving an oral summary of the three stages of culture shock with your partner.

AFTER THE LECTURE

SHARING YOUR OPINION

1 | Work in a small group. Read the list of behaviors below. Discuss whether these behaviors are acceptable in your community? Why or why not?

  1 Kissing your friends two or three times on alternating cheeks when you greet them

  2 Holding hands with a person of the same sex when you walk in the street

  3 Eating or drinking in the street

  4 Pointing at someone with your forefinger

  5 Crossing your legs in public

2 | In your group, discuss the kinds of behavior that a person visiting your community should know about. What is considered acceptable or unacceptable?

Gender Roles

In this unit you will hear people talk about gender roles. Chapter 3 deals with the issues that boys and girls face as they grow up. You will hear an interview with a mother about how she is trying to raise her son, and an interview with a young man who discusses how he, his brother, and his sister were raised. You will also hear a lecture on single-sex education and the benefits it can offer girls. In Chapter 4, you will hear interviews with a woman and a man about gender equality at home and at work. The lecture in Chapter 4 is about issues of gender and language.

Chapter 3

Growing Up Male or Female

1 GETTING STARTED

In this section you are going to discuss the concept of gender and how children learn gender roles. You will also listen to nursery rhymes that children in English-speaking countries learn when they are young, and think about how these rhymes depict boys and girls in traditional gender roles.

READING AND THINKING ABOUT THE TOPIC

1 | Read the following passage.

Biology determines what *sex* we are at birth – that is, whether we are male or female. However, society and culture determine our *gender roles* – that is, the socially learned patterns of behavior that distinguish boys from girls and men from women. Gender roles are learned through the process of socialization. In other words, we learn what society considers masculine and feminine as we grow up and interact with other people.

Becoming a man or woman is dramatically more complex now than it was a century ago. Boys and girls today have more freedom to explore their individuality and less pressure to conform to traditional gender roles. For example, today both young men and young women can have jobs that were previously limited to only one sex. Children who are born today are given choices about the way males and females should behave and think. Many of today's gender roles were unthinkable in our parents' or grandparents' generations.

2 | Answer the following questions according to the information in the passage.
   1 How do we learn about masculinity and femininity?
   2 How have gender roles changed?

3 | Read these questions and share your answers with a partner.
   1 When you were a child, what did your family, teachers, or friends tell you about men's and women's behavior?
   2 Do you think that gender roles will continue to change in the future? How?

PERSONALIZING THE TOPIC

1 | Read the following list of personality traits. First, match the trait with the correct description. Then decide whether you believe these qualities are *mostly biological* (things you are born with) or *mostly social* (things you learn). For each trait, check (✔) the appropriate box. Then compare your answers with a partner.

Description	Personality Trait	Mostly Biological	Mostly Social
Gets along well with other people	Athletic	☐	☐
Is good at sports	Brave	☐	☐
Can make decisions alone	Competitive	☐	☐
Is not afraid of doing things	Cooperative	☐	☐
Wants to be the best at things	Friendly	☐	☐
Does what he or she wants to do	Independent	☐	☐
Prefers to be led by others	Mischievous	☐	☐
Is afraid to talk to others; is shy	Passive	☐	☐
Works well with other people	Strong-willed	☐	☐
Behaves badly	Timid	☐	☐

2 | Now work as a group. Look at the list of traits below and write a short description for each one. Do you think that these traits are mostly biological or mostly social?

adventurous	aggressive	cowardly	gentle	helpful
kind	nice	responsible	sweet	thoughtful

⌒ BUILDING BACKGROUND KNOWLEDGE ON THE TOPIC

1 | Work in a small group. Look at the pictures below. These pictures illustrate some nursery rhymes – traditional children's songs and poems – that are taught to children in many English-speaking countries. Describe what is happening in each picture.

1 What Are Children Made Of?

2 Jack Be Nimble

3 Polly, Put the Kettle On   **4** Little Miss Muffet   **5** Georgie Porgie

2 | Now listen to the nursery rhymes. In the chart below, write the personality traits from "Personalizing the Topic" that describe the girl(s) or boy(s) in each rhyme. You do not have to use all the traits and you may use some more than once. ▶ PLAY

Rhymes	Personality Traits	
	Girls	**Boys**
1		adventurous
2		
3	helpful	
4		
5	timid	

3 | Share your answers with your group. Discuss how these rhymes characterize girls and boys. Do you think these characterizations are accurate?

2 AMERICAN VOICES: Linda and Shingo

In this section you will hear two people discuss the ways that boys and girls are raised. First, Linda talks about how she has tried to bring up her son. Then Shingo, a 26-year-old man from Japan who is living and studying in the United States, compares his and his brother's upbringing with that of his sister.

BEFORE THE INTERVIEWS

PERSONALIZING THE TOPIC

1 | As boys and girls grow up, they are usually given chores – small jobs – to do around the house, but these chores are often assigned by gender. Think about yourself and your friends. As children, who was asked to help their parents with the chores listed below: boys, girls, both, or neither? For each chore, check (✔) the appropriate column.

Who was asked to . . .	Boys	Girls	Both	Neither
take out the garbage?	☐	☐	☐	☐
wash the dishes?	☐	☐	☐	☐
iron?	☐	☐	☐	☐
sew buttons on clothes?	☐	☐	☐	☐
clean the house?	☐	☐	☐	☐
cook meals?	☐	☐	☐	☐
repair household items?	☐	☐	☐	☐

2 | In your community, what kind of behavior is encouraged among young girls and boys (under the age of 10)? For each behavior, check (✔) the appropriate column.

Toys **Who is encouraged to play with . . .**	Boys	Girls	Both	Neither
balls?	☐	☐	☐	☐
dolls?	☐	☐	☐	☐
trucks?	☐	☐	☐	☐
crayons and paints?	☐	☐	☐	☐

Games **Who is encouraged to . . .**	Boys	Girls	Both	Neither
play "house" (pretend to do household chores)?	☐	☐	☐	☐
play "mommies and daddies"?	☐	☐	☐	☐
play sports?	☐	☐	☐	☐
dress up in costumes?	☐	☐	☐	☐

Clothes	Boys	Girls	Both	Neither
Who is encouraged to wear . . .				
pink clothes?	☐	☐	☐	☐
blue clothes?	☐	☐	☐	☐
pants or overalls?	☐	☐	☐	☐
shorts?	☐	☐	☐	☐
jewelry?	☐	☐	☐	☐

3 Share your answers to steps 1 and 2 with a partner. Which answers were the same? Which were different?

INTERVIEW WITH LINDA: *Bringing up a son*

Here are some words and phrases from the interview with Linda printed in **bold** and given in the context in which you will hear them. They are followed by definitions.

the most **critical issue** is: *important problem*

They're expected to **excel** in sports: *do extremely well*

There's a major **bonding** that goes on: *feeling of closeness and friendship*

They still **tease** each other very **harshly** and **relentlessly**: *make fun of* **/** *in a rough way* **/** *without taking a break*

Roles were **prescribed**: *already decided by society, unchangeable*

I want him to be financially **stable**, but not necessarily **wealthy**: *secure, safe* **/** *rich*

🎧 ANSWERING MULTIPLE-CHOICE QUESTIONS

When answering multiple-choice questions, read the directions carefully before you begin. Are you being asked to choose one answer or two? Must you choose the *correct* answer or the *incorrect* answer?

1 In this interview, Linda talks about her goals for her teenage son. Before you listen, read the items and possible answer choices below. For each item, *two* answers are correct and *one* is incorrect.

1 Linda wants her son to be
  a proud of himself.
  b good to his parents.
  c sensitive.

2 Boys are expected to
  a be tougher.
  b be better at sports.
  c form groups easily.

3 Men use sports as
  a the basis for social relationships.
  b something to talk about.
  c a way to relate to women.

4 Many people say that boys are closed emotionally. Linda thinks that boys
  a are *very* closed emotionally.
  b share a lot of their intimate feelings with other boys.
  c are more open than they used to be in the past.

5 In Linda's view, boys are scared of
  a not being big enough.
  b not being accepted.
  c not being intelligent enough.

6 In society in the past,
  a roles were prescribed.
  b there was more flexibility.
  c jobs often gave lifetime employment.

7 Linda would like her son to be
  a rich.
  b a good friend.
  c a caring member of society.

Linda

2 | Now listen to what Linda says and choose your answers. **▶ PLAY**

3 | Compare your answers with a partner.

INTERVIEW WITH SHINGO: Growing up as a boy or girl

Here are some words and phrases from the interview with Shingo printed in **bold** and given in the context in which you will hear them. They are followed by definitions.

They **shelter** her more: *take closer care of*

They didn't mind that I wouldn't be that **close**: *geographically near*

I don't want to be **restricted**: *limited*

The boys did **woodwork**: *carpentry*

But nowadays, there is less **discrimination**: *unequal treatment*

If they need a lot of my **support**, I'll give it to them: *emotional or physical help*

You have to be **flexible**: *able to change according to the situation*

Shingo

∩ LISTENING FOR SPECIFIC INFORMATION

1 | Read the following statements before you listen to the interview. Each statement refers to a way that parents can treat their children.

Parents can . . .

_____ **1** care about their children.

_____ **2** give them independence and let them do what they want.

_____ **3** allow them to study in other countries.

_____ **4** want them to live nearby after they marry.

_____ **5** spend a lot of time with them.

_____ **6** take them shopping.

_____ **7** pay for what they want to buy.

_____ **8** teach them how to cook.

2 | Now listen to the interview. Write *S*, *D*, *B*, or *N* in the blank next to each statement in step 1. ▶ **PLAY**

S (sons):   the way Shingo's parents treated their sons

D (daughter):   the way Shingo's parents treated their daughter

B (both):   the way both the sons and the daughter were treated

N (neither):   The statement doesn't apply to either the sons or the daughter.

3 | Compare your answers with a partner and then discuss any differences as a class.

AFTER THE INTERVIEWS

DRAWING INFERENCES

Drawing inferences means understanding things that are not directly stated by a speaker. When you listen to people speak, you should not only think about what they tell you directly, but you should also be aware of what they communicate indirectly. Drawing inferences is a critical aspect of listening.

1 | For each of the following statements, decide whether you think it correctly reflects what Linda or Shingo inferred in their interviews. Write *T* next to the statement if you think it is true or *F* if you think it is false.

1 Linda probably thinks that

_____ **a** it isn't easy for girls to make friends if they aren't good at sports.

_____ **b** boys today communicate with each other better than they did in the past.

_____ **c** it is difficult for boys to grow up in today's changing world.

_____ **d** both boys and girls should be caring members of society.

2 Shingo probably thinks that

_____ **a** parents want their daughters to stay closer to them than their sons.

_____ **b** schools should offer the same classes to boys and girls.

_____ **c** parents love their sons and daughters in different ways.

_____ **d** children should not be allowed to make their own decisions.

2 | Work with a partner. Check to see if you drew the same inferences. Explain why you thought each answer was true or false. You may disagree about your answers.

SHARING YOUR OPINION

1 | Look at the following photographs. They show people of both sexes in roles that were unusual for their gender in the past.

2 | Discuss the photographs with a partner. How common would these scenes be in your community?

3 IN YOUR OWN VOICE

In this section you will conduct some research on gender issues and present your findings to the class. You will also practice responding to presentations.

CONDUCTING AND PRESENTING YOUR OWN RESEARCH

Academic lecturers and textbooks often refer to research conducted by experts. It is useful to try to copy the experts' research experiments on a smaller scale. Doing your own research will give you an idea of some of the steps involved in doing extensive research. It can also provide interesting information and lead to unexpected findings.

1 | Read some background information.

Many researchers have reported on the kinds of behavior we expect from men and women. In one experiment, Nielsen et al. made a list of behaviors that are commonly seen in public among men or women. Then they found male students who were willing to act as volunteers and behave in "female" ways, and female students who were willing to act like "males." They secretly followed the volunteers around and took notes on the way other people reacted to them.

2 | Prepare your own experiment.

Look at the list of behaviors below. With a partner, decide if each behavior is commonly associated with men or women. In the blank following each behavior, write *M* (male) or *F* (female).

- Giving a bouquet of roses to a member of the opposite sex _____
- Knitting or sewing _____
- Having painted fingernails or toenails _____
- Reading a romance novel _____
- Carrying a handbag _____
- Talking about cars or sports, such as boxing or football _____
- Opening doors for a member of the opposite sex _____
- Crying quietly and drying your eyes with a tissue _____
- Other (your own example) _____ _____
- Other (your own example) _____ _____

3 | Conduct your experiment.

Divide into groups so that each group has some male and some female students. Each group should pick two of the behaviors listed in step 2 and conduct the experiment. Some group members will be the actors while the others should record the reactions of onlookers. For example, if you decided that giving a bouquet of roses to a member of the opposite sex is an activity normally associated with males, have a female actor give roses to a male actor. Do this in a public place. Make it look natural. The other students in your group will be watching nearby and will take notes about the reactions of onlookers.

4 | Present your findings.

Choose one or two members of your group to tell the class what happened during your experiment. Did the actors' behavior provoke any strong reactions, or did it go unnoticed? What did your experiment show you about the behavior we expect to see among men and women? Do any of your results surprise you? You may want to review the guidelines for giving an oral presentation on page 9.

RESPONDING TO PRESENTATIONS

When your classmates make oral presentations, listen to them carefully. Many professors will expect you to respond by asking questions and making comments at the end of a presentation. If you make it a habit to think critically about what each presenter says, you will be able to respond intelligently. Your response will help both you and the presenter think more deeply about the topic.

1 | Make a chart similar to the one below that you can use to take notes on your classmates' presentations. Fill out a chart for each presentation.

Title of presentation: _____	
Presenter's name: _____	
Content of the presentation	**Your questions and comments**
What did the experiment consist of? What were the results?	

2 | As you listen to each presentation, take notes on the content.

3 | After each presentation is over, take a few minutes to write your questions and comments.

4 | Share your questions and comments with each presenter.

4 ACADEMIC LISTENING AND NOTE TAKING: The Benefits of Single-Sex Education for Girls

In this section you will hear and take notes on a two-part lecture given by Dr. Mary Frosch, a teacher and advisor at an all girls' school. The title of the lecture is *The Benefits of Single-Sex Education for Girls.* Dr. Frosch will explain why girls seem to learn better when boys are not around.

BEFORE THE LECTURE

BUILDING BACKGROUND KNOWLEDGE ON THE TOPIC

1 | Read the following report about research done in coeducational classrooms.

> Various studies carried out in coeducational schools have shown that in many of these classrooms teachers interact differently with boys and girls. To begin with, it is clear that there are many more teacher-student interactions with male students – in other words, boys get more attention from their teachers. This could be because, in general, boys are more aggressive. One study reported that boys are eight times more likely than girls to call out answers in class.
>
> Another way that teachers treat the sexes differently in coed settings is that they tend to give boys more demanding academic challenges than girls. Boys are expected to be problem solvers, to think for themselves, and to explain their answers. Girls, on the other hand, are often just corrected if they make mistakes and are encouraged to be quiet and well behaved. They are rarely asked follow-up questions and are called on for answers much less frequently than boys.

2 | Answer the following questions with a partner.

1 What does the term *coeducational* mean? Check a dictionary if necessary.

2 According to the passage, what are the differences between the ways girls and boys are treated in coeducational classes?

3 Are boys and girls treated differently by teachers in coeducational schools that you have attended? If so, how?

3 | Compare your ideas with other students in the class.

∩ NOTE TAKING: USING SYMBOLS AND ABBREVIATIONS

When you are taking notes during a lecture, you have to write down a lot of information very quickly. Instead of writing out each word separately, you should develop the habit of using symbols and abbreviations.

You may want to change some of the symbols and abbreviations below to ones that are easier for you to remember and use. You will probably also want to invent some of your own, depending on the content of the lecture you are attending. When you invent symbols and abbreviations, it is important to review your notes as soon as possible after the lecture while their meanings are still fresh in your mind.

Symbols

Here are some symbols that are commonly used in English. Many of them come from the field of mathematics.

&	(and)	**=**	(is the same as, means, equals)
. . .	(and so on, etc.)	**≠**	(is different from, doesn't mean)
@	(at)	**<**	(is less than)
∴	(therefore)	**>**	(is more than)
+	(plus, in addition to)	**"**	(ditto, as said before, similarly)
#	(number)	**→**	(causes, leads to, results in)
$	(dollars)	**%**	(percent)

Abbreviations

In addition to using symbols, good note takers abbreviate long words or words that are frequently used. Here are a few standard abbreviations that are commonly used in English. Notice that some are based on Latin words.

Ex. or **e.g.**	(for example; "e.g." is from the Latin *exempli gratia*)
w/	(with)
etc.	(and other similar things, from the Latin *etcetera*)
A.M.	(before noon, from the Latin *ante meridiem*)
P.M.	(after noon, from the Latin *post meridiem*)
gov't	(government)
ed.	(education)
Prof.	(Professor)
Dr.	(Doctor)
usu.	(usually)

Pro and *Con*

pro	(for, a Latin prefix meaning "in favor of")
con	(against, an abbreviation of the Latin *contra*)

When taking notes, these two words are useful. Many texts and lecturers talk about arguments for or against something, or the advantages and disadvantages of something. In such cases, it is easy to simply use the heading *pro* for arguments in favor of something or its advantages, and the heading *con* for arguments against something or its disadvantages. (The terms may be used in the plural as well: *pros* and *cons*.) It is also common for people to use these terms in conversation.

1 | Study the symbols and abbreviations in the column on the left. Match them with their definitions in the column on the right. You might want to use some of these symbols and abbreviations in your notes for the lecture in this chapter.

_____ **1** ♂   **a** single-sex education

_____ **2** ♀   **b** coeducation, coeducational

_____ **3** ed   **c** boy

_____ **4** ben(s)   **d** different

_____ **5** s-s ed.   **e** against, disadvantage

_____ **6** →   **f** opportunities

_____ **7** pro   **g** recommend

_____ **8** opps   **h** and

_____ **9** . . .   **i** benefit(s)

_____ **10** coed   **j** girl

_____ **11** diff   **k** for, in favor of

_____ **12** rec.   **l** education, educational

_____ **13** &   **m** causes, leads to, results in

_____ **14** con   **n** and so on, etc.

2 | Compare your answers with a partner.

3 | Now listen to an excerpt from the lecture. Take notes as you listen, using symbols and abbreviations. Use your notes to tell your partner what you heard. Did you gather the same information? ▶ **PLAY**

LECTURE, PART ONE: Disadvantages and Advantages of Single-Sex Education for Girls

GUESSING VOCABULARY FROM CONTEXT

1 | The following items contain important vocabulary from Part One of the lecture. Work with a partner. Using the context and your knowledge of related words, take turns trying to guess the meanings of the words in **bold**.

_____ **1** I'm often asked to **defend** single-sex education.

_____ **2** as if girls' schools were **on trial**

_____ **3** goes against the aims and the goals of **feminists**

_____ **4** Single-sex schools do not provide a **smooth transition** into the adult world.

_____ **5** Single-sex education **values** girls.

_____ **6** It values girls' **unique** qualities.

_____ **7** It helps girls develop **self-confidence**.

2 Work with your partner. Match the vocabulary terms with their definitions by writing the letter of each definition below in the blank next to the sentence or phrase containing the correct term in step 1. Check your answers in a dictionary if necessary.

    a unusual, special
    b easy way
    c the feeling that you can manage any situation
    d being questioned in a court of law
    e people who support women's rights
    f encourages and supports
    g explain why I am in favor of

NOTE TAKING: USING SYMBOLS AND ABBREVIATIONS

1 Look at these notes on Part One of the lecture. Think about what kind of information might belong in the blanks. Notice that these notes are formatted in columns. The *Cons* (disadvantages, reasons against) are in the first (left) column because these are the first aspects of the topic that Dr. Frosch presents. The *Pros* (advantages, reasons in favor of) are in the second (right) column. Putting your notes in columns labeled *Pros* and *Cons* is often an effective way to organize notes if a lecture is an argument for or against something, which this lecture is.

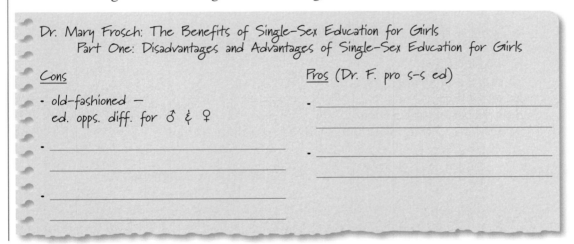

Dr. Mary Frosch: The Benefits of Single-Sex Education for Girls
    Part One: Disadvantages and Advantages of Single-Sex Education for Girls

Cons   Pros (Dr. F. pro s–s ed)

- old-fashioned —
  ed. opps. diff. for ♂ & ♀

2 Now listen to Part One of the lecture. Take notes on your own paper. Remember to use symbols and abbreviations. ▶ **PLAY**

3 Use your own notes to complete the notes in step 1.

4 Compare your completed notes for step 1 with a partner.

LECTURE, PART TWO: Two Main Benefits of All Girls' Schools

GUESSING VOCABULARY FROM CONTEXT

1 | The following items contain important vocabulary from Part Two of the lecture. Work with a partner. Using the context and your knowledge of related words, take turns trying to guess the meanings of the words in **bold**.

_____ 1 Girls can often concentrate on higher-level, **abstract** thinking.

_____ 2 Girls also enjoy **collaborative** learning activities and so they work well in groups.

_____ 3 Girls become more self-confident without the **distraction** of boys.

_____ 4 If they do not understand a concept, they will ask for **clarification**.

_____ 5 When girls are in the same classrooms as boys, they often lose their **self-esteem**.

_____ 6 Girls typically **sink back** in their chairs and wait for the boys to quiet down.

_____ 7 Perhaps they can change the "real" world into a place designed to **accommodate** both women and men.

2 | Work with your partner. Match the vocabulary terms with their definitions by writing the letter of each definition below in the blank next to the sentence containing the correct term in step 1. Check your answers in a dictionary if necessary.

a done with other people; joint
b respect for themselves
c explanations
d make a place for
e sit timidly
f conceptual, theoretical
g something that takes away your attention; disturbance

⌖ NOTE TAKING: USING YOUR NOTES TO WRITE A SUMMARY

Summarizing is an essential study skill. It means reducing a whole lecture (or part of a lecture) to a few sentences. A good summary shows that you have understood what the lecture is about and what the most important points are. It is a helpful record for you to review when you are studying for a test.

During the lecture, take notes in whatever way works best for you. After the lecture, revise your notes as soon as possible by making sure they are in a clear format and by adding any missing information. Then use your notes to help you write your summary. Reread your notes and select the most important points that the lecturer made. Write a summary in which you explain the main points in your own words.

1 | Listen to Part Two of the lecture and take notes in whatever way works best for you. Remember to use symbols and abbreviations. ▶ **PLAY**

2 | Organize your notes in an appropriate format. Do you want to put your notes into columns as you did for Part One? Do you think an outline form would be better? (See "Note Taking: Organizing Your Notes in Outline Form," pages 27–28.) Or do you have another way that you would like to organize your notes?

3 | Compare your notes for steps 1 and 2 with a partner.

4 | Following is a summary of Part Two of the lecture. Use your notes to complete the summary. You may need to put more than one word in some blanks. Then compare summaries with your partner. Do you have similar answers? You don't have to use exactly the same words because summaries are in your *own* words.

The Benefits of Single-Sex Education for Girls
Part Two: Two Main Benefits of All Girls' Schools
Dr. Mary Frosch

Single-sex education _____ girls' unique qualities and also helps girls develop _____.
   The unique qualities of girls include their ability to concentrate on _____ thinking at an _____ age than boys and their ability to _____ for longer periods of time. They also enjoy working in groups and teams. Girls are not as competitive as boys, but they tend to be _____.
   Boys can be noisy and girls often react by becoming timid and losing their _____. When they learn without the _____ of boys, girls feel confident in themselves, they enjoy being _____, they help each other, and they freely ask for _____ if they don't understand something. In single-sex schools, girls can develop deep confidence in themselves. This self-confidence prepares them to become adults.

AFTER THE LECTURE

THINKING CRITICALLY ABOUT THE TOPIC

> One way to practice thinking critically about an issue is to argue both in favor of it and against it. After doing this, you may find that you still strongly hold your original opinion, or you may find that you have changed your mind.

1 | Look at the statements below. Put an *A* in front of each statement that you agree with. Put a *D* in front of each statement that you disagree with.

_____ **1** The idea of having separate schools for boys and girls is old-fashioned.

_____ **2** Some girls are just as aggressive as boys are.

_____ **3** If you put adolescent boys and girls together, they concentrate more on each other than they do on their classes.

_____ **4** Girls work together much better if there are no boys around.

_____ **5** Boys can get very loud in class and then they get all the teacher's attention.

_____ **6** Boys and girls don't work well together.

_____ **7** It is more natural to have coed schools.

2 | Work in a group of three students. Take turns in the "hot seat." If it is your turn, explain why you agree with one of the statements in step 1. The other two students should strongly disagree with the statement you are defending. Think of as many arguments for and against each statement as possible. Here are some ways to express disagreement or to ask for clarification:

Expressing disagreement	*I'm not sure if I agree with you because . . .*
	I'm afraid that I disagree with you because . . .
	I don't agree with your explanation of . . . because . . .
	I think that you're wrong because . . .
Asking for clarification	*Excuse me – are you saying . . . ?*
	I'm sorry, but I don't understand what you mean when you say (that) . . .
	Can you explain that again?
	Can you give us some more information about . . . ?
	Why do you think that . . . ?

3 | Discuss as a class whether or not you changed your opinion about any of the statements in step 1 as a result of your discussions in step 2.

Gender Issues Today

Chapter 4

1 GETTING STARTED

In this section you are going to discuss changes in traditional gender roles. You will also listen to a conversation about gender stereotypes, which are fixed ideas about what men and women are like.

READING AND THINKING ABOUT THE TOPIC

1 | Read the following passage.

> During the twentieth century, the feminist movement became more active. Women made a great deal of progress toward gaining equal opportunities in education. More and more women also entered the workforce. Both girls and boys were encouraged to choose careers they wanted and didn't feel that they had to choose careers that were traditional for their gender. At home, husbands and wives began to share household chores and caring for children.

These changes in gender roles have helped women make progress toward gaining equal rights in many areas of life. However, sociologists agree that the problem of gender inequality is still a serious issue facing society today.

2 Answer the following questions according to the information in the passage.
   1 How did women's lives change in the twentieth century?
   2 How did men's lives change in the twentieth century?
   3 What do sociologists believe about gender inequality today?

3 Read these questions and share your answers with a partner.
   1 How have women's roles changed since your parents' or grandparents' generation?
   2 How have men's roles changed since your parents' or grandparents' generation?
   3 Can you think of an example from your own experience of inequality between men and women?

EXAMINING GRAPHIC MATERIAL

1 Look at the chart below that shows the percentages of jobs held by women in various professions in 1975 and in 2000:

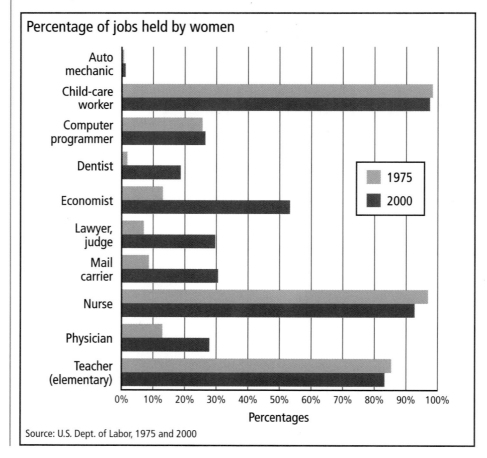

Percentage of jobs held by women

Source: U.S. Dept. of Labor, 1975 and 2000

2 | Discuss the following questions with a partner.

    1 In which fields did women make the most gains between 1975 and 2000?

    2 What information in the chart particularly surprises or interests you?

🎧 LISTENING FOR SPECIFIC INFORMATION

1 | Read the beginning of a conversation between Jack and Sheila, a married couple. They are discussing an article Jack read about gender stereotypes.

Jack:	Hey, Sheila, I just finished reading an interesting article about gender inequality in the workplace. It's by Natasha Josefowitz.
Sheila:	What does she say?

Jack:	Well, she talks about common situations that happen to employees who work in offices. Here are some of them:
	  1 The employee is going to get married.
	  2 The employee has a family picture on his or her desk.
	  3 The employee is talking with a coworker.
	  4 The employee is going to go on a business trip.
	Then she says that coworkers react differently depending on whether the employee in the situation is a man or a woman.

Sheila:	You mean that people react differently if, for example, the person getting married is a man or a woman? Tell me what the article says.
Jack:	OK. Let me see what I can remember . . .

2 | Discuss the following question with a partner:

    How do you think people react differently to the situations Jack mentions if the employee is a man or a woman? Why?

3 | Listen to what Jack remembers about the situations in the article. Take notes on your own paper. ▶ PLAY

4 | Compare your notes for step 3 with your partner. Did you understand the same things?

2 AMERICAN VOICES: Belinda and Farnsworth

In this section you will hear Belinda, a successful American entertainer and filmmaker, describe her feelings about discrimination against women in the workplace. Then you will hear Farnsworth, a social worker who helps people with emotional problems, give his views on gender discrimination at home and in the workplace.

BEFORE THE INTERVIEWS

BUILDING BACKGROUND KNOWLEDGE ON THE TOPIC

1 | *Metaphors* are words that give visual pictures of ideas and make the ideas easier to understand. Read the following list of metaphors about the workplace and their definitions. Discuss any words that you don't understand with other classmates. Check a dictionary if necessary.

   a Glass ceiling: The glass ceiling is the invisible barrier that women often "hit" as they try to get promoted to higher positions within a company.

   b Glass escalator: The glass escalator is the invisible machine that seems to promote men to higher positions.

   c Sticky floor: The sticky floor is the force that seems to hold women back in less important and lower paid positions.

   d Old boys' club: This refers to the all-male groups that men form and the connections they make with each other to help themselves gain power and success.

   e Mommy Track: People often think that working women with children are not serious about their jobs. They say that these women are on the "Mommy Track." That is, they are not on the road – or "track" – that leads to higher positions.

   f Level playing field: The level playing field is like a sports field in which all the players are on the same level and have the same chance to win. Having a level playing field means that no one group has more opportunity to succeed than any other group.

2 | Match each of the following situations with one of the metaphors in step 1. Write the letter of the metaphor next to the situation.

_____ **1** A woman talking to her friend about her boss:
"Since my baby was born, my boss looks at me strangely every time I get sick and take a day off. I'm sure he thinks that I just want to stay home with my baby."

_____ **2** A sales manager talking to another sales manager who was just hired:
"Don't worry, Sam, we'll help you with your new position. What about getting together with some of the guys after work tonight?"

_____ **3** A company director talking to a personnel manager:
"We need to hire a new office assistant. Be sure to tell the people you interview that all employees are encouraged to apply when higher positions become available."

_____ **4** Two employees talking about a third employee:
"He's gone from sales clerk to assistant manager to manager in eighteen months. That's a record!"

_____ **5** An excerpt from a business report:
"There are about fifty female Executive Vice Presidents in the largest companies, but only two female Chief Executive Officers."

_____ **6** A woman talking to her friend:
"Even though I have good skills, everywhere I go, I seem to get offered the lowest paid positions."

3 | Discuss the following questions in a small group.

1 Do you think that the metaphors listed in step 1 give an accurate picture of the problems that women face in the workplace?

2 Can you give any examples of these metaphors from your own experience?

INTERVIEW WITH BELINDA: Gender discrimination in the workplace

Here are some words and expressions from the interview with Belinda printed in **bold** and given in the context in which you will hear them. They are followed by definitions.

The first answer is yes – that's my **gut** feeling: *deep and immediate*

There's this "old boys' club," the **support network** that men have: *groups and connections*

I have **mixed feelings**: *feelings that are in conflict with each other*

Sometimes I think that I'm just **making excuses for myself**: *finding reasons not to feel bad about myself*

It's **cool** for everyone to be successful: *OK*

🎧 ANSWERING MULTIPLE-CHOICE QUESTIONS

Belinda

1 | Read the following questions before you listen to Part One of the interview. Which answer do you think is probably correct?

1 The interviewer asks Belinda if she has ever been discriminated against because she is a woman. Belinda answers:

    a Yes.

    b No.

    c Yes and no.

    d Not sure.

2 The question that Belinda asks herself is:

    a Should I talk to my boss about getting promoted?

    b Am I as good as the men?

    c Would I be making more progress if I were male?

    d What would my brother do in my position?

3 Belinda's feeling about the current situation in the workplace is that

    a there has been no progress toward gender equality.

    b women should form their own support groups.

    c there is more opportunity for women today than in the past.

    d women will never have gender equality.

4 Belinda thinks that women

    a usually think about themselves more than men do.

    b help themselves and other people, too.

    c work much harder than men.

    d can't make a place for themselves in the business world.

2 | Now listen to the interview. Take notes on what Belinda says. Use your notes to choose the best response for each question in step 1. Circle one choice for each question. ▶ **PLAY**

3 | Compare your answers with a partner.

INTERVIEW WITH FARNSWORTH: Gender inequality at home and in the workplace

Here are some words and expressions from the interview with Farnsworth printed in **bold** and given in the context in which you will hear them. They are followed by definitions.

a **pay disparity**: *difference in pay*

The changes in the last twenty years have been **relatively modest**: *not very large or important*

Ninety percent of my **colleagues** are women: *coworkers*

both the **CEO** and his boss: *chief executive officer – one of the most important positions in a company*

Men are raised with **a sense of entitlement**: *a feeling that they deserve the best opportunities*

if they are divorced and have **custody**: *legal responsibility for a child*

Women just **assume that they can do it**: *feel that they can do it even though they haven't done it before*

I joined **a playgroup** with my son: *a group of mothers and/or fathers that meets so that their children can play together*

He wasn't really **an active parent**: *a parent who is physically involved in caring for his or her children*

ᑑ ANSWERING TRUE/FALSE QUESTIONS

When answering true/false questions, read all parts of each statement carefully. Some parts of a statement may be true, but if any part of it is false, then the whole statement is false. Pay special attention to statements with negatives in them. These statements are often tricky. Remember that a negative statement that is correct is true.

1 | Read the following statements before you listen to the interview with Farnsworth.

_____ **1** Farnsworth believes that there is real equality between men and women now.

_____ **2** Women make as much money as men do, so the "pay disparity" that used to exist doesn't exist anymore.

_____ **3** Farnsworth believes that the glass ceiling exists because at his job most of the higher paid positions are held by men.

_____ **4** Farnsworth believes that there is much more equality between the sexes at home. Men and women tend to share the housework.

Farnsworth

_____ **5** Farnsworth wishes he had been more active in raising his children. He thinks he should have helped out more when they were babies with tasks like giving them a bottle at night and cooking.

_____ **6** Farnsworth says that when divorced men get custody of their children, they often don't feel that they can take good care of the children.

_____ **7** When his son was small, Farnsworth joined a children's playgroup. He was the only man involved in this activity.

2 | Now listen to the interview. Write *T* (true) or *F* (false) next to each of the statements in step 1. ▶ **PLAY**

3 | Compare answers with a partner and then with the class. Correct the false statements together.

AFTER THE INTERVIEWS

THINKING CRITICALLY ABOUT THE TOPIC

1 | Belinda and Farnsworth talk about the increase in the number of women who work and the increase in the number of men who want to be active parents. One result of these social changes is that new types of arrangements have to be worked out for child care. Read the following problem situations. Discuss a possible solution to each problem with a partner, preferably someone of the opposite sex. Make notes about your solutions.

1 A divorced father has custody of three young children. When they get sick and cannot go to school, he has to use his own sick days – days that employees are allowed to take off if they are sick – so that he can stay home from work and take care of them.

Possible solution: Employers could allow employees with children a certain number of "sick child days" per year in addition to their own personal sick days.

2 A company often asks its employees to do overtime, that is work longer than the normal workday. One employee doesn't want to do overtime because she wants to spend evenings with her children.

Possible solution: _____

_____

_____

3 A young father would like to spend time with his newborn baby. He requests a six-month leave of absence without pay. The company tells him that they cannot guarantee that he will get his job back after the leave.

Possible solution: _____

_____

_____

4 An employee has a new baby. She needs to make more money so that she can afford child care because she and her husband both work.

Possible solution: _____

_____

_____

2 | Share your solutions with the class. Are other students' solutions similar to or different from yours and your partner's?

EXAMINING GRAPHIC MATERIAL

1 Look at the graph below. It shows the "gender gap" in pay that is one of the most important issues for working women today.

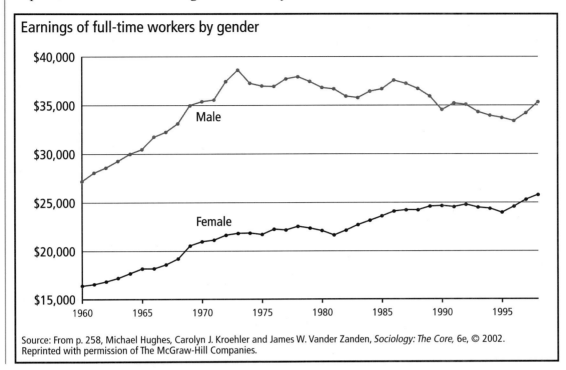

Earnings of full-time workers by gender

Source: From p. 258, Michael Hughes, Carolyn J. Kroehler and James W. Vander Zanden, *Sociology: The Core,* 6e, © 2002. Reprinted with permission of The McGraw-Hill Companies.

2 Work with a partner. Take turns describing what the graph in step 1 shows about:

1 the difference between men's and women's salaries

2 how this difference is changing over time

You can use these sentence structures to discuss the graph:

There was a	big / significant	increase / rise decrease	in X	in	YEAR.
X		rose / increased fell / decreased		between	YEAR and YEAR.
Compared to DATE,		women / men		now	X.

3 What do you think are some factors that cause women to earn less than men?

3 IN YOUR OWN VOICE

In this section you will interview a few men and women about the issues that active fathers face today. You will begin by gathering some background information on the topic. After your interviews, you will present your findings to the class and give each other feedback on your presentations.

CONDUCTING AN INTERVIEW

An interview is a meeting in which someone who wants to learn more about a topic asks questions of another person – usually a person who has personal knowledge of the topic. Conducting interviews can be a useful way for students to increase their knowledge. An interview will be more successful if the interviewer gathers background information about the topic beforehand and uses this information to prepare questions.

1 | Read the following information about the "Mommy Track" and the "Daddy Track."

You have probably heard the expression "Mommy Track." This refers to the problems that mothers often face as they try to juggle family and work responsibilities. For example, women with children who do not want to work overtime may not get promoted to high positions.

However, as more and more fathers take an active role in the care of their children, they are finding that they face similar problems. This phenomenon is called the "Daddy Track." For example, if fathers take some time off work after their children are born – this time off is called *paternity leave* – they might be criticized by their boss or their colleagues and not get promoted.

2 | Work with a partner and gather background information about the problems that active fathers face today. You can do this through the resources of a library, such as encyclopedias or other reference books and textbooks, or through an Internet search. Here are some "keywords" that you could type into an Internet search engine to get started.

- Daddy Track
- paternity leave
- promotions
- dependent children
- fathers and child care
- (Add two or three of your own keywords.)

Here are some examples of the kind of information you might look for:
- the percentage of men who stay at home with their children while their wives work
- the problems men face at work because they want to be active parents
- the problems men face at home because they want to be active parents
- the similarity between the problems facing women on the Mommy Track and men on the Daddy Track

3 Use the information you found in step 2 to prepare questions for your interviews. Here are some examples:

> *Who stays with your children during the day?*
> *How active are you as a father?*
> *Do you have problems at work because you are an active parent? What kinds of problems?*
> *Is it true that . . . ?* (add something you read about in your research)
> *Do you agree that . . . ?* (add something you read about in your research)

4 Interview at least three people outside of class and take notes on what they say. Try to arrange interviews with working men and women who have children. Organize your findings and present them to the class.

GIVING FEEDBACK ON A PRESENTER'S STYLE

Remember that when you listen to other students make presentations, you should think critically about what they have to say. Sometimes, you may also be asked by your professor to give constructive feedback on the presenter's style. This will help both you and the presenter think about what makes a good presentation and, therefore, improve your presentation skills. Good presentations are well prepared, clearly organized, and effectively delivered.

1 Make a chart that you can use to take notes on your classmates' presentations. Your chart might look something like the one below. Fill out a chart for each presentation.

Title of presentation: _____

Presenter's name: _____

Preparation and organization	Delivery
Is the speaker well prepared? (If not, what could be improved?)	Does the presenter speak loudly and clearly?
	Does the presenter look at the audience?
Are the ideas clearly organized? (If not, what could be improved?)	Does the presenter use effective visual aids? (If not, do you think visual aids would improve the presentation?)

2 Share your feedback with each presenter. If you think a presentation could be improved, try to think of constructive suggestions for the presenter.

4 ACADEMIC LISTENING AND NOTE TAKING: Gender and Language

In this section you will hear and take notes on a two-part lecture given by Wendy Gavis, a professor of linguistics. The title of the lecture is *Gender and Language.* Professor Gavis will discuss how to avoid sexism in language, and will respond to students' questions.

BEFORE THE LECTURE

BUILDING BACKGROUND KNOWLEDGE ON THE TOPIC

1 | Read the following paragraphs from a book about gender-specific and gender-neutral language.

When speaking or writing, it is important that you avoid using gender-specific terms wherever possible because these terms can show *sexism* – that is, prejudice and discrimination based on a person's gender. The term *chairman,* for example, is often used to refer to a person who is the leader of a meeting, a committee, or an organization. But *chairman* implies that the position is always held or can only be held by a man. Instead, a gender-neutral term such as *chair* or *chairperson* can be used. Similarly, a term like *woman doctor* should be avoided since a doctor can be male or female.

In English, it is difficult to be gender-neutral when using pronouns. Grammatically, "a good doctor submits his reports on time" is correct. However, so is "a good secretary types his letters on time" and "a good shopper always does his shopping before the crowds arrive."

2 | Discuss the following questions with a partner.

1 What is a "gender-specific" term? Can you think of some examples?

2 What is a "gender-neutral" term? Can you think of some examples?

3 Why is it difficult to be gender-neutral when using pronouns?

4 What do the pronouns used in the second paragraph of the reading imply about the doctor, the secretary, and the shopper?

⌒ NOTE TAKING: USING TELEGRAPHIC LANGUAGE

When you listen to a lecture, it is not possible to write down everything the lecturer says. Good note takers are able to write down the most important information in as few words as possible. Using *telegraphic language* will help you to do this quickly.

Telegraphic language is abbreviated language that reads like newspaper headlines.

When you use telegraphic language, you usually don't include the following:

Articles (*a, an,* and *the*)
The verb *to be* and other linking verbs
Prepositions and pronouns

Look at this example of telegraphic language:

Original sentences

The first topic I will discuss is the large increase in the number of students who attend college today compared with the past. There has been a large increase of both male and female students.

Telegraphic language

Topic 1: Large incr. in # of Ss in college today compared to past — ♂ & ♀.

Notice that the note taker has also used abbreviations and symbols. Using telegraphic language together with symbols and abbreviations will help you to become a good note taker.

1 Read the following summaries of different parts of the lecture.

_____ **a** The topic of today's lecture is sexism in language and how to avoid it.

_____

_____ **b** There are a great many gender-specific terms. Words like *mailman* or *policeman* are gender-specific because they only refer to men.

_____

_____ **c** The word *mankind* sounds as if you are only talking about men, but when you say *human beings* or *people*, then you include both men and women.

_____

_____ **d** The words we use affect how we think. For example, if children grow up hearing *chairman*, they think the title must always refer to a man.

_____

2 Now listen to the four short excerpts and match them with the correct summaries. Write the number of each excerpt in the correct blank in step 1. ▶ **PLAY**

3 On the line underneath each summary in step 1, rewrite the summary in telegraphic language. Use symbols and abbreviations whenever you can.

LECTURE, PART ONE: Gender-Specific and Gender-Neutral Language

GUESSING VOCABULARY FROM CONTEXT

1 The following items contain important vocabulary from Part One of the lecture. Work with a partner. Using the context and your knowledge of related words, choose the best synonym for the words in **bold**.

_____ **1** You **get my point**, right?
    a understand me   **b** agree with me   **c** aren't sure

_____ **2** A safe **option** is to use what we call "gender-neutral" terms.
    a method   **b** probability   **c** choice

_____ **3** Children **internalize** the idea that all leaders are men.
    a reject   **b** question   **c** get

_____ **4** I'm facing a **dilemma**.
    a controversial topic   **b** difficult choice   **c** hard fact

2 | Compare your answers with a partner. Check your answers in a dictionary if necessary.

🎧 NOTE TAKING: USING TELEGRAPHIC LANGUAGE

1 | Look at these notes on Part One of the lecture. Notice how the note taker uses telegraphic language, symbols, and abbreviations. (Review the list of symbols and abbreviations in "Note Taking: Using Symbols and Abbreviations," page 43, if necessary.) Read the notes and think about what kind of information might belong in the blanks.

> Prof. Wendy Gavis: Gender and Language
> Pt 1: Gender-specific and gender-neutral language
>
> I Main idea: _____
>
> II Gen-spec. lang.
>   A Def: _____
>   B Ex:
>   1 mail   <u>man</u>
>   2 _____   "
>   3 _____   "
>
> III _____ lang. shows
>   A World as is — ♀ can have same jobs as ♂ (Ex: _____ &
>   _____ & _____)
>   B Equality (Ex: _____)
>
> IV _____
>   A Choices
>   1 Everyone pick up <u>his</u> pen.
>   2 " " " __ ".
>   3 _____
>   B Gavis uses _____ – not gram., but solves prob.
>   C _____

2 | Now listen to Part One of the lecture. Take notes on your own paper using telegraphic language. Use symbols and abbreviations wherever you can. **▶ PLAY**

3 | Use your own notes to complete the notes in step 1.

4 | Compare the notes you took on your own paper and your completed notes for step 1 with a partner.

LECTURE, PART TWO: Questions and Answers

GUESSING VOCABULARY FROM CONTEXT

1 | The following items contain important vocabulary from Part Two of the lecture. Work with a partner. Using the context and your knowledge of related words, take turns trying to guess the meanings of the words in **bold**.

_____ **1** the **AIDS** crisis

_____ **2** the way the **mass media** treats women

_____ **3** the way they **stereotype** women

_____ **4** The language question is also **on the minds of** international organizations.

_____ **5** The girls just stand **in the background**.

_____ **6** By focusing on the language we use about women, we may be able to change their **expectations**.

_____ **7** Does this **controversy** exist in other languages, too?

_____ **8** It is definitely receiving more attention **worldwide**.

2 | Work with your partner. Match the vocabulary terms with their definitions by writing the letter of each definition below in the blank next to the sentence or phrase containing the correct term in step 1. Check your answers in a dictionary if necessary.

    a channels of communication – such as television, radio, and newspapers – that reach large numbers of people

    b ideas that we have about the way people should behave

    c in a position of less importance

    d everywhere in the world

    e Acquired Immune Deficiency Syndrome – a very serious disease

    f being considered by

    g present a fixed, narrow idea of what they are like

    h debate, dilemma

⌒ NOTE TAKING: USING TELEGRAPHIC LANGUAGE

1 | Read the following questions about gender and language. Think about the kind of information you might hear in response to these questions.

1 There are many very serious gender issues facing society today. How important is the language question?

2 If we change the way we talk about people, does that mean we change the way we think about them?

3 Does gender-specific language occur in other languages besides English? Does the same controversy exist everywhere about using gender-neutral language?

2 | Now listen to Part Two of the lecture. Take notes on your own paper using telegraphic language. Use the questions in step 1 as a guide to help you listen for the important points. ▶ **PLAY**

3 | Work with a partner. Looking at the telegraphic language you and your partner have used, take turns answering the questions in step 1 orally.

AFTER THE LECTURE

APPLYING WHAT YOU HAVE LEARNED

Finding ways to apply what you have learned is a good way to deepen your understanding of new subject matter.

"Blivens, how would you like to be a member of the old boy's club?"

1 | Look at the cartoon. What is it saying? How does it relate to the lecture?

2 | Read the following excerpt from a student's essay. Notice how difficult it is for the student to use pronouns correctly. Rewrite the paragraph using plural nouns and pronouns where appropriate. In this way, you can avoid sexism and also avoid using *he/she, his/her,* or *him/her.* You may also need to change verbs to agree with the subject. Compare your completed paragraph with two other classmates.

> According to an article I just read, the quality of a university does not just depend on the ~~teacher~~ teachers, but on the student. The teacher has to make sure his/her lessons are challenging and stimulating. But the student is also responsible for doing her homework, bringing her ideas to the classroom discussions, and contributing her opinions on the topic. He/she must make sure that he is not being passive, but are making full use of the opportunities that are being offered to them at the university. For example, the student should be ready to join clubs and participate with her/his classmates on special projects. He/she can also learn a lot by having a job that will bring him into contact with all the members of the university. These activities also contribute to a successful college experience.

Media and Society

This unit is about the mass media and its effects on our lives. Chapter 5 concerns the news coverage provided by the media. You will hear interviews with three people about the strengths and weaknesses of the news we get from television, radio, and the newspaper. In the lecture, a journalist gives her insight into how an event becomes a news story. In Chapter 6, you will hear people discuss the positive and negative effects of various forms of the media. The lecture is about the dangerous effects the media can have on us.

Chapter 5

Mass Media Today

1 GETTING STARTED

In this section you are going to discuss the mass media and think about what makes news interesting and relevant to our lives.

READING AND THINKING ABOUT THE TOPIC

1 Read the following passage.

The modern world depends on extensive communication between people, organizations, and governments. Rapid transportation and electronic communication have shortened the distances between us, and most of us are now aware of what is going on in places far away. Much of our new awareness comes from the mass media, including newspapers, magazines, movies, TV, and the Internet, which allows information to be communicated quickly throughout the world.

However, the rapid growth in the mass media sometimes raises questions about its value. For example, although we get more information and news from the mass media than ever before, some people believe that today's news is not necessarily of good quality. Technological advances have given us the impression that we understand the world better because we have access to more information about it. But this is not always true. The information we get may be inaccurate, one-sided, or incomplete.

2 Answer the following questions according to the information in the passage.

1 How is the modern world connected?

2 What does the mass media allow us to do?

3 Why do some people question the value of the mass media?

3 Read these questions and share your answers with a partner.

1 What kinds of mass media do you use most?

2 Do you think that the quality of the news we get from newspapers, radio, TV, and the Internet is good? Why or why not?

3 Do you believe that technology helps us understand the world better than we used to? Why or why not?

🎧 LISTENING FOR SPECIFIC INFORMATION

1 Read the headlines below. Then listen to the news stories that correspond to the headlines. Choose the headline that goes with each story by writing the number of the story next to its headline. **▶ PLAY**

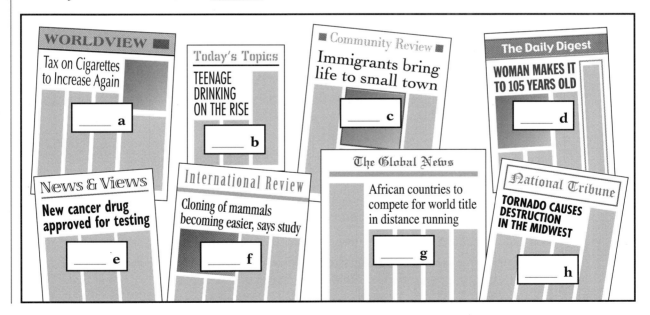

2 Compare your answers with a partner.

3 If the headlines in step 1 appeared in a newspaper you were reading, which stories would you read first? Why? Discuss your answers with your partner.

2 AMERICAN VOICES: Carol, Shari, and Frank

In this section you will hear three people discuss different perspectives on the news. Carol, a teacher, will explain her mixed feelings about the news she watches on TV. Shari, a student in her twenties, and Frank, a retired postal worker, will discuss their reactions to the news they read in the newspaper.

BEFORE THE INTERVIEWS

SHARING YOUR OPINION

1 | Look at the following chart. In each column, circle the word or words that best describe your answer to the question.

1 How interested are you in the news?	2 Where do you get most of your news?	3 Which aspects of the news interest you most?	4 What do you think of the quality of the news?	5 How do you think the news should be improved?
Extremely interested	TV	Current events	Excellent	Make it more international
Somewhat interested	Internet	Stories about people	Fair	Make it less sensational
Not very interested	Newspapers	Sports or entertainment	Bad	Make it less negative
Not sure (explain)	Other (explain)	Other (explain)	Not sure (explain)	Other (explain)

2 | Discuss your responses with a partner and explain your opinions. Which questions prompted similar answers? Where did you disagree?

INTERVIEW WITH CAROL: Problems with TV News

Here are some words and phrases from the interview with Carol printed in **bold** and given in the context in which you will hear them. They are followed by definitions.

The news is based on what's going to keep people **tuned in**: *watching TV*

People are interested in **plastic surgery** or **celebrities**: *medical surgery to improve your physical appearance / famous people*

Find out how this woman **lost weight**: *became thinner*

It's **shallow**: *without serious meaning*

There are these people **doing voice-overs**: *speaking "off-camera" about what the viewer is watching*

It's **equating** those types of information: *giving equal value to*

Like a **sitcom**: *TV series in which the same characters appear week after week (abbreviation for "situation comedy")*

It's like **instant gratification**: *immediate satisfaction*

TV news has to be reported by **news anchors** who are physically attractive: *the main news reporters on TV*

Do you think newspapers give you better **coverage**?: *reporting*

I know I'm being **sucked in**!: *tricked into watching*

⌒ ANSWERING MULTIPLE-CHOICE QUESTIONS

1 Read the questions below before you listen to the interview with Carol.

Carol

1 According to Carol, news on TV
  a is mostly about health issues.
  b is mostly international.
  c is mostly entertainment.

2 In Carol's opinion, the evening news
  a is boring to most people.
  b tricks people into watching.
  c is an important source of information.

3 Carol thinks that political problems
  a don't get reported in the way they should be reported.
  b are not really interesting for most people.
  c are presented well by TV reporters.

4 Carol believes that most people
  a are very interested in war and politics.
  b want information quickly.
  c don't watch the news.

5 Carol says that if TV news anchors are not physically attractive,
  a people will not watch TV news.
  b viewers will complain.
  c viewers will change channels.

6 According to Carol, newspapers
  a have a wider audience than TV.
  b can be read quickly.
  c have the same problems as TV.

7 Carol feels that news on the Internet
  a is worse than the TV.
  b is hard to find.
  c is too general.

8 Carol
  a almost never watches the news on TV.
  b watches TV news even though she doesn't think it's good.
  c avoids the mass media.

2 | Now listen and circle the one correct answer for each question. ▶ **PLAY**

3 | Work with a partner and discuss your answers. Do you agree with Carol?

INTERVIEW WITH SHARI AND FRANK: *Reading the newspapers*

> Here are some words and phrases from the interview with Shari and Frank printed in **bold** and given in the context in which you will hear them. They are followed by definitions.
>
> The news is really **depressing**: *unhappy and without hope*
>
> It's **a prestige thing** to cover the international news: *something done to look important*
>
> The human interest stories can be really **uplifting**: *positive, inspirational*
>
> It was shocking that the **judicial** system had failed: *legal*
>
> I read the main stories, especially the **scandals**: *shocking stories about people who have committed crimes or immoral acts*
>
> You have to **take it with a grain of salt**: *not believe all of it*
>
> It's a lot of **half-truths**: *stories that are partly true and partly false*
>
> It's really **biased**: *presented from only one point of view, one-sided, not objective*

🎧 LISTENING FOR SPECIFIC INFORMATION

1 | Work with a partner. Read the description of Shari and Frank and the ten statements below before you listen to the interviews. Try to predict who might have these opinions. Write *S* (Shari) or *F* (Frank) under "Your prediction."

Shari is a young Korean woman who is now living and attending graduate school in the United States. Frank retired from his job at the post office in 1993 at the age of 65.

	Your prediction	Fact
1 I get most of my news on the Internet.	____	____
2 I like to read the newspaper every day.	____	____
3 I usually start with the front page.	____	____
4 I like to turn to the culture section.	____	____
5 I was interested in a story about a crime in the park.	____	____
6 I turn to the sports and find out how my teams are doing.	____	____
7 I love to do the crossword puzzles.	____	____
8 I'm interested in international news.	____	____
9 You have to use your own ideas in order to analyze the news.	____	____
10 The news in the United States focuses too much on negative events.	____	____

2 Now listen to the interview. Write *S* (Shari) or *F* (Frank) under "Fact." Compare answers with your partner and then with the class. ▶ PLAY

Shari

Frank

AFTER THE INTERVIEWS

PARAPHRASING WHAT YOU HAVE HEARD

Read the following paraphrase of the interviews with Carol, Shari, and Frank. Fill in the blanks using information from the interviews. You may need more than one word in some blanks. Compare paraphrases with a partner. They do not have to be exactly the same.

Carol has very strong opinions about the news we get on _____.
She thinks that it is more like _____ than news. For
example, serious stories about _____
and shallow stories, like _____, are
presented in the same style. She believes that this is because we are used to
instant _____ – something that doesn't require you to
_____. Newspapers and the Internet give better coverage,
but it takes more time to find good articles, so Carol _____
_____.

    Shari gets her news from _____ and _____.
She thinks that the news is very _____. For example, there
are stories about bombings and _____. She also says that
news in the United States is not as _____ as it is in Korea.
Her favorite sections are arts and culture and she likes to read about
_____.

    Frank likes the newspaper. His favorite parts are _____
and _____. He thinks you have to have your own
_____ about the news, because it is usually
_____.

SHARING YOUR OPINION

1 | Discuss the following questions in a small group.

  1 Do you think people will continue to read newspapers, or do you think the Internet will take their place?

  2 Do you think that the Internet and TV have a positive or negative effect on our ability to read and our pleasure in reading?

  3 Do you think that you watch too much TV? Why or why not?

  4 Do you like listening to news on the radio? Why or why not?

  5 How many hours each week do you spend on the Internet? What do you use the Internet for?

  6 Do your parents use the same media as you do to get the news? If not, which type of media do they use? Why?

2 | Look at the cartoon below. Discuss with your group what you think Carol, Shari, and Frank might say about it.

"*I'm sorry, Mel, but we're letting all our anchormen go. Our viewers don't want any more news.*"

3 IN YOUR OWN VOICE

In this section you will discuss important events of the twentieth century. Then you will work in groups to discuss what makes a news event important and you will share your ideas with the class by giving group presentations.

GIVING GROUP PRESENTATIONS

Sometimes college professors ask students to give group presentations on a topic. To do this effectively, everyone in the group should work together as a team and contribute to the success of the project. Here are some guidelines:

- Choose one person to be a coordinator. The coordinator should make sure that each person in the group has different responsibilities and that the work is distributed equally.
- Gather enough background information to make your presentation interesting and convincing.
- Make an outline of what you want to say and prepare an introduction.
- Divide your ideas so that each person has something different to say.
- Practice your presentation together several times before you give it in class.

1 Work as a class. Read the following clues about events that the American public and journalists selected as top news stories of the twentieth century in a recent survey. Guess what event is being described. (Check your answers at the bottom of page 74.) Then discuss why you think the event was – or was *not* – important.

1903   Two men did something that people thought was impossible.

Event: _The Wright brothers flew an airplane._

1 1905   A scientist developed a theory that changed our idea of the universe.

Event: _____

2 1912   There was a big accident at sea.

Event: _____

3 1920   Women took a big step toward gaining equal rights.

Event: _____

4 1928   An antibiotic was discovered.

Event: _____

5 1929   There was a financial crisis in the United States.

Event: _____

6 1945   The United States used a weapon that had never been tried before.

Event: _____

7 1963   A famous political leader was assassinated.

Event: _____

8 1969 Explorers took a great step into the unknown.

Event: _____

9 1989 A new form of mass media was invented.

Event: _____

10 1997 Scientists made a clone of a mammal.

Event: _____

2 | Work with a small group and decide what *you* consider important since 1900. For each category listed below, write an event or the name of a person that was important in relation to the category.

1 War or political change: _____

2 Exploration: _____

3 Scientific discovery: _____

4 Accident: _____

5 Disease: _____

6 Other: _____

7 Other: _____

8 Other: _____

3 | Prepare a group presentation to give to the class on one of the following topics:

- An event, discovery, or person from the twentieth century that everyone in the group decides was very important. Present as many details as you can about your selection and explain why it was important.

- An event, discovery, or person in the news today that you think will be considered important in the future. Explain in detail the significance of the person, discovery, or event.

4 | Practice your presentation and then present it to the class.

Answers to step 1, pages 73–74

1 Albert Einstein developed the theory of relativity. **2** The "unsinkable" ship Titanic sank. **3** Women in the United States won the right to vote. **4** Penicillin was discovered. **5** The U.S. stock market crashed. **6** The United States dropped the atomic bomb. **7** U.S. President John F. Kennedy was assassinated. **8** A human being walked on the moon for the first time. **9** The World Wide Web was invented. **10** Dolly, a sheep, was cloned.

4 ACADEMIC LISTENING AND NOTE TAKING: From Event to Story – Making It to the News

In this section you will hear and take notes on a two-part lecture given by Ms. Sarah Coleman, a journalist. The title of the lecture is *From Event to Story – Making It to the News*. Ms. Coleman will explain the steps journalists take and the difficulties they face as they write the stories we read in the newspaper.

BEFORE THE LECTURE

PERSONALIZING THE TOPIC

People often discuss the role of newspapers in society, and they frequently disagree about what newspapers should and should not do. Discuss the following questions with a partner.

1 What is a newspaper's role? Should newspapers give us only information, or opinions too?

2 Should journalists write a story even if they do not have all the facts or if they are not sure that all the facts are correct?

3 What do you think is the most difficult thing about a journalist's job?

THINKING CRITICALLY ABOUT THE TOPIC

1 Read the guidelines for responsible journalism below. Then with a partner, choose an event that happened recently in your community or country. Find two or three articles about the event in different newspapers. Analyze each article using the guidelines.

- Do not tell lies – only tell the truth.
- Do not include unnecessary details – only include details that directly affect the story.
- Do not use sensationalism to make the story more interesting.
- Be fair and present all sides of the story.
- Do not confuse news and entertainment.

2 One of the issues that the public faces is how to know if the information that appears in newspapers is accurate. Discuss the following questions with your partner in relation to the articles you read for step 1. Support your answers.

1 How do you know the journalists wrote the truth?

2 How do you know if they were fair and presented all sides of the story?

🎧 NOTE TAKING: LISTENING FOR SIGNAL WORDS

When you are reading a text, you can see how it is organized because it is divided into paragraphs. It may also have section headings. You can also read a text slowly, underline parts you do not understand, and come back to them later.

In a lecture, it is more difficult to follow the organization of the speaker's ideas. However, signal words can help you. These words act as markers or signposts that indicate what kind of information the speaker will give next. In Chapter 1, you learned signal words for introducing examples and definitions. Signal words can be used for other purposes, too. Here are some examples of commonly used signal words:

To indicate time	*today, nowadays, sometimes, usually, at that point*
To reinforce an idea or introduce a contradiction	*in fact, actually*
To list ideas	*first of all, then, after that, finally*
To introduce a new idea	*and, also, in addition, furthermore*
To introduce an opposite idea	*but, however, on the other hand*

1 | The signal words in the left column are used by the lecturer. Read them and match each one with a synonym from the column on the right. Fill in each blank with the correct answer.

_____ **1** Sometimes   **a** These days

_____ **2** First of all   **b** But

_____ **3** In fact   **c** Occasionally

_____ **4** Nowadays   **d** Generally

_____ **5** However   **e** To begin with

_____ **6** Usually   **f** Actually

2 | Now listen to some parts of the lecture that include the signal words in step 1. As you listen, fill in the blank with the correct word(s). Then compare your answers with a partner. ▶ PLAY

1 _____, more than ever before, we are surrounded by news.

2 _____, so many new stories appear every day that it's impossible to keep up with them!

3 _____, there are different kinds of journalists.

4 _____, journalists are called reporters because they "report" the news.

5 _____, unplanned events are more exciting!

6 _____, it's important not to report too much personal information or anything that is scandalous.

LECTURE, PART ONE: The Work of a Journalist

GUESSING VOCABULARY FROM CONTEXT

1 │ The following items contain important vocabulary from Part One of the lecture. Work with a partner. Using the context and your knowledge of related words, take turns trying to guess the meanings of the words in **bold**.

_____ **1** So many new stories appear every day that it's impossible to **keep up with** them.

_____ **2** She should keep in contact with **civic organizations** in the neighborhood.

_____ **3** The reporter can **anticipate** many of the details.

_____ **4** The reporter will probably see a few lines about the crime in the **police log**.

_____ **5** She can begin to interview **witnesses**.

_____ **6** These details will make the story more **credible**.

_____ **7** It's important not to report anything that is **scandalous**.

_____ **8** She will go back to the **newsroom** to write the story.

_____ **9** She might talk to her **editor** to decide whether she has a good story.

2 │ Work with your partner. Match the vocabulary terms with their definitions by writing the letter of each definition below in the blank next to the sentence containing the correct term in step 1. Check your answers in a dictionary if necessary.

a supervisor of reporters
b groups of citizens who organize activities to help and improve the neighborhood
c read all of, stay informed about
d know in advance
e people who see a crime happen
f shocking, related to scandals
g easy to believe
h office at a newspaper where news is prepared for publication
i record of crimes

⌒ NOTE TAKING: CHOOSING A FORMAT FOR ORGANIZING YOUR NOTES

Remember that you do not always have time to choose the best format for organizing your notes clearly when you are listening to a lecture. If the notes you took during a lecture are disorganized, choose an appropriate format and put your notes into that format as soon after the lecture as possible. It is important to have clear notes so that they are useful tools with which you can study. The more you practice taking notes, the easier it will be to choose an appropriate format for them while you listen.

1 | Look at the three examples of notes on Part One of the lecture below. Example 1 is an example of a student's disorganized notes on Part One of the lecture. They were taken while the lecturer was speaking. Examples 2a and 2b show two different ways that the same information can be organized into clear formats. Example 2a is in column form and Example 2b is in outline form.

Example 1: Disorganized notes of Part One of the lecture, "The Work of a Journalist," that were taken by a student during the lecture

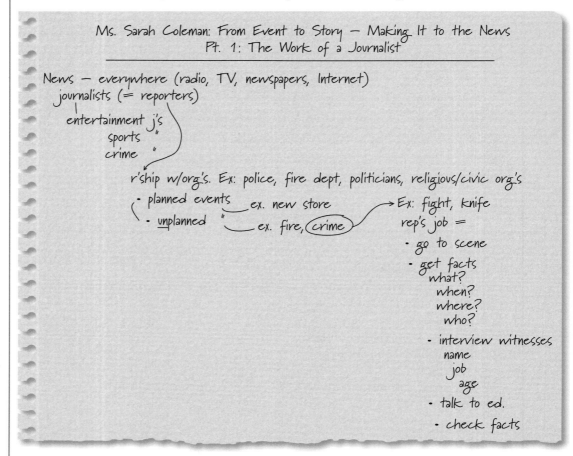

Example 2a: The first part of notes clearly organized in column format based on the information in Example 1

Example 2b: The first part of notes clearly organized in outline format based on the information in Example 1

Ms. Sarah Coleman: From Event to Story — Making It to the News
Part One: The Work of a Journalist
I   News everywhere: radio, TV, newspapers, Internet
II Journalists report news
    A diff' types of journalists (reporters)
        1 entertainment
        2 sports
        3 crime
    B J's establish r'ship w/org's
        1 police/fire depts.
        2 politicians
        3 relig/civic org's

2 | Now listen to Part One of the lecture and take notes on your own paper. Pay attention to the signal words to help you follow the lecture. ▶ **PLAY**

3 | Decide whether you want to organize your notes for Part One of the lecture in column format or outline format. Then, complete the notes in Example 2a (column format) or 2b (outline format) by adding information from the notes you took in step 2.

LECTURE, PART TWO: Getting a Story into Print

GUESSING VOCABULARY FROM CONTEXT

1 | The following items contain important vocabulary from Part One of the lecture. Work with a partner. Using the context and your knowledge of related words, take turns trying to guess the meanings of the words in **bold**.

_____ **1** whether or not the story is **accurate**

_____ **2** The public would have been **misinformed**.

_____ **3** Bill Jones could decide to **sue** the paper for misrepresenting his character.

_____ **4** That's called **libel**, and it's something judges take very seriously.

_____ **5** Every controversial fact should be supported by two different **sources**.

_____ **6** There must be no **uncorroborated** facts.

2 | Work with your partner. Match the vocabulary terms with their definitions by writing the letter of each definition below in the blank next to the sentence containing the correct term in step 1. Check your answers in a dictionary if necessary.

a given incorrect information

b unchecked

c correct, true

d the crime of telling untrue stories about a person

e bring a legal case against

f people or documents from which you get information

🎧 NOTE TAKING: CHOOSING A FORMAT FOR ORGANIZING YOUR NOTES

1 | Now listen to Part Two of the lecture and take notes on your own paper. Pay attention to the signal words to help you follow the lecture. ▶ **PLAY**

2 | Complete your organized notes for the lecture by adding information about Part Two to the column or outline format you chose for Part One. Then compare your notes with a partner.

AFTER THE LECTURE

APPLYING WHAT YOU HAVE LEARNED

1 | Work as a class. Choose a day when you will all buy the same edition of the same newspaper. Read the paper before you go to class.

2 | In small groups, analyze the following sections of the newspaper. Decide how good you think each section is. Circle the word that best describes your opinion of the quality of each section.

Section	Quality		
1 International news	excellent	good	not very good
2 Local or national news	excellent	good	not very good
3 Arts / Entertainment	excellent	good	not very good
4 Sports	excellent	good	not very good

3 | Compare your opinions and give reasons for your choices. You can use these phrases in your discussion:

To begin to say something	*I have something to say . . .*
	I would like to make a comment . . .
	I want to point something out . . .
To agree with someone	*I agree with X . . .*
	I think the same as X . . .
	Yes, that's right . . .
To disagree with someone	*I disagree with X . . .*
	I have a different idea . . .
	Yes, but think about this . . .

The Influence of the Media

1 GETTING STARTED

In this section you are going to think about the positive and negative influences of the media. You will also take notes on statistical information about television ownership.

READING AND THINKING ABOUT THE TOPIC

1 | Read the following passage.

> The media has become one of society's most important agents of socialization. Television, radio, newspapers, the Internet, and other forms of media have a strong effect on the way we think and act. However, there is disagreement about exactly what the effect is. For example, access to television allows us to be better informed and gives us an increased understanding of the world. TV can also be used to entertain us. However, television exposes us to negative images, too. Furthermore, some critics argue that it may make us passive, violent, or too materialistic.
>
> Other forms of mass media, such as video games, magazines, and movies, may influence our ideas strongly, too. We do not yet really understand the extent of their impact on society.

2 | Answer the following questions according to the information in the passage.

   1 Does everyone agree about the kind of effects the media has on society?

   2 What are some positive effects of TV? What are some negative effects?

3 | Read these questions and share your answers with a partner.

   1 Do you watch a lot of TV? Are you concerned about its possible negative effects? Explain.

   2 What steps do you think parents, schools, and the government should take to protect children and adolescents from the negative effects of on-screen violence?

   3 Of all the forms of media mentioned in the paragraph, which one seems to have the most influence on you? Why?

PERSONALIZING THE TOPIC

1 | What kind of entertainment do you enjoy? Fill in the chart below.

Media	Details
TV	Three programs you watch:
Magazines	Three magazines you read:
Songs	Three songs you like:
Movies	Three movies you have enjoyed:
Radio	Three stations you listen to:
Internet	Three sites you visit:
Other?	

2 | Share your responses with a small group.

🎧 RECORDING NUMERICAL INFORMATION

> It will often be necessary to record the numerical information you hear in conversations, interviews, or lectures. Practice by visualizing numbers when you hear them and then writing them down quickly.

1 | TV is one of the most popular and influential forms of mass media in the world. Work with a partner. Look at the map below that highlights four areas of the world. Guess how many TVs per one hundred people you think each area has. Write your guess in the blank next to each area.

Area 1: _____   Area 2: _____   Area 3: _____   Area 4: _____

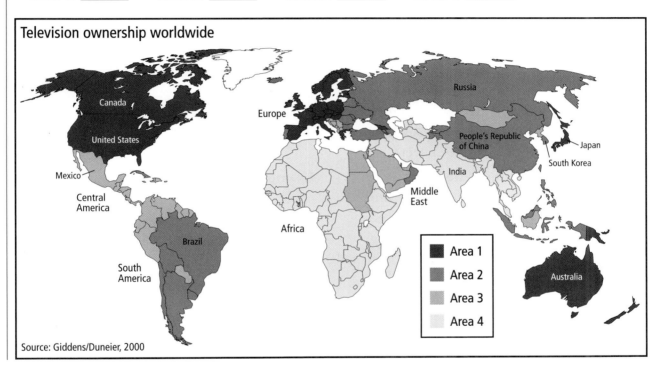

Television ownership worldwide

Source: Giddens/Duneier, 2000

2 | Listen to a report on television ownership in each of the four areas of the world in the map in step 1. Write the number of televisions per one hundred people next to the area being described. ▶ **PLAY**

Area 1: _____   Area 2: _____   Area 3: _____   Area 4: _____

3 | Compare your answers to step 2 with your partner. Then compare those answers with your guesses in step 1.

4 | Discuss the following questions in a small group.

1 What information in the report surprises you? Why?

2 In which areas of the world do you think TV has the most influence on people? Why? How do you think it influences them?

2 AMERICAN VOICES: Eddie, Leslie, Ralph, Vanessa, Felix, and Richard

In this section you will hear six people of different ages give their opinions about the positive and negative effects of various forms of media.

BEFORE THE INTERVIEWS

PERSONALIZING THE TOPIC

1 | Work with a partner and read the following positive and negative effects of the media. Discuss each effect and find an example that you and your partner agree about. Write the examples in the blanks.

Positive effects	Example
Keeps the user well informed	*Newspapers tell us what is happening in the world.*
Is entertaining	_____
Is a good use of time	_____
Is a good form of communication	_____
Allows users to share opinions	_____
(Other positive effect)	_____

Negative effects	Example
Causes users to waste time	_____
Encourages violence	_____
Has too much advertising	_____
Encourages people to think alike	_____
(Other negative effect)	_____

2 | Now look at the forms of media below. Choose three. Explain to your partner the positive and negative effects each one has on you.

- Television
- Video games
- Magazines
- Internet
- Telephone
- Newspapers
- Movies
- Other?

INTERVIEW WITH EDDIE, LESLIE, AND RALPH: Opinions about media

Here are some words and phrases from the interview with Eddie, Leslie, and Ralph printed in **bold** and given in the context in which you will hear them. They are followed by definitions.

Eddie

maybe a **wasteful** effect: *something that makes you use time badly*

Video games **restrict** the things kids do: *limit*

Do big kids know the difference between **fantasy** and reality: *something in your imagination, not real*

The reason is not because they'll make you **deranged**: *crazy, mentally disturbed*

Violent games . . . just make the kid **a little bit more antisocial**: *less friendly*

Leslie

I used to think they were just **trendy**: *the latest fashion*

a **status symbol** thing: *sign of being rich or important*

She is able to **keep tabs on us**: *know where we are*

Ralph

You've got to **keep an eye on** the movies your children watch: *pay attention to*

You've got to **check out** the program: *become familiar with*

Eddie

Leslie

Ralph

🎧 LISTENING FOR SPECIFIC INFORMATION

1 Work with a partner. Read the descriptions of the people who were interviewed in the left column. Then listen to parts of their interviews. Write the form of media they are discussing in the right column. ▶ **PLAY**

Person	Type of media
Eddie is 15 years old. He is interested in sports, music, and traveling.	_____
Leslie is 24 years old. She is currently studying to become a teacher.	_____
Ralph is 40 years old. He is a plumber and electrician.	_____

2 Now listen to the entire interview with these three people. As you listen, take notes on the positive and negative effects of the form of media each person is discussing. Write your notes in the chart on page 86. ▶ **PLAY**

Person	Positive effects	Negative effects
Eddie		
Leslie		
Ralph		

3 | Compare your notes with your partner.

INTERVIEW WITH VANESSA, FELIX, AND RICHARD: Opinions about media

Here are some words and phrases from the interview with Vanessa, Felix, and Richard printed in **bold** and given in the context in which you will hear them. They are followed by definitions.

Vanessa

It's completely **drained of** all real information: *without, empty of*

[News is influenced by] the **corporate and political interests**: *powerful corporations and political groups*

The news is totally **manipulated**: *controlled*

anything that is not **prepackaged**: *prepared in advance*

Felix

Sports give you a lot of **character**: *good qualities*

I like a good **whodunit**: *mystery movie (from the words "Who done it?")*

Parents are the **nucleus** of the family: *center*

Especially when the kids are in their **formative** years: *young age when good or bad qualities are developed*

Richard

You have to look at the **trade-off**: *disadvantages*

I **link up with** people: *communicate*

Vanessa

Felix

Richard

🎧 LISTENING FOR SPECIFIC INFORMATION

1 | Work with a partner. Read the descriptions of the people who were interviewed in the left column. Then listen to parts of their interviews. Write the form of media they are discussing in the right column. ▶ **PLAY**

Person	**Type of media**
Vanessa is 44 years old. She is a musician.	_____
Felix is 65 years old. Now retired, he is building a house in Florida.	_____
Richard is 75. He lives in a large city and loves to travel.	_____

2 | Now listen to the entire interview with these three people. As you listen, take notes in the chart below on the positive and negative effects of the form(s) of media each person is discussing. Sometimes more than one form of media is discussed. ▶ **PLAY**

Person	Positive effects	Negative effects
Vanessa		
Felix		
Richard		

3 | Compare your notes with your partner.

AFTER THE INTERVIEWS

DRAWING INFERENCES

Remember that when you listen, you should try to be aware of what people communicate indirectly, or infer, when they speak.

1 | Decide whether you think the following statements correctly reflect what the people who were interviewed inferred. Write *T* (true) or *F* (false) next to each statement.

_____ **1** Eddie believes that video games can be entertaining.

_____ **2** Eddie doesn't like to waste time.

_____ **3** Leslie would not buy something because it was trendy.

_____ **4** Leslie thinks that there are no good reasons to have cell phones.

_____ **5** Ralph thinks that children should not watch TV.

_____ **6** Ralph thinks that parents should monitor all their children's activities.

_____ **7** Vanessa gets all her news by watching TV.

_____ **8** Vanessa thinks that it's a good idea to make the news entertaining.

_____ **9** Felix believes that girls should be encouraged to participate in sports.

_____ **10** Felix thinks that children should only watch educational programs.

_____ **11** Richard enjoys writing letters.

_____ **12** Richard has a fax machine.

2 | Work with a partner. Check to see if you drew the same inferences. Explain why you thought each statement was either true or false. You may disagree about your answers.

THINKING CRITICALLY ABOUT THE TOPIC

Work in a small group. Choose three of the following statements to discuss. Explain why you agree or disagree with each statement. Give examples to support your opinions.

1 The violence in video games has a very bad effect on teenagers.

2 Cell phones are essential items for today's world.

3 Young children cannot understand the difference between imaginary things and real things.

4 TV news is a good way to stay well informed.

5 Parents should closely monitor their children's TV viewing habits.

6 Modern machines and technology destroy a lot of the beauty in life.

3 IN YOUR OWN VOICE

In this section you will conduct an experiment about television that was designed by the sociologist Bernard McGrane of Chapman University. It is called "The Un-TV Experiment."

CONDUCTING AND PRESENTING YOUR OWN RESEARCH

1 Read about how to conduct "The Un-TV Experiment."

The Un-TV Experiment

You are going to watch TV for three ten-minute periods. In each of these periods, you will watch a different TV program and do a different task. You will take notes about the tasks. You should sit very quietly and concentrate completely on what you are doing so that you do not make a mistake as you record your data. Make sure that you have everything you need: a comfortable place to sit and write, a pencil or pen, and enough paper.

The Tasks

1 Watch any TV program for ten minutes. Count how many times you see a technical manipulation (that is, a change) on the screen, including:

- a cut (the picture changes to another picture, like a slide show)
- a fade-in or fade-out (one picture slowly changes into another picture)
- a zoom (the camera moves from a wide view to a close-up view, or from a close-up view to a wide view)
- a voice-over (a voice explains or comments on what you are watching)
- another technical change (describe it)

2 Watch a news program for ten minutes.

- Count the number of positive images that you see.
- Count the number of negative images that you see.

Make notes about any images that you particularly remember.

3 Watch any TV program for ten minutes. Do not turn on the sound. As you watch, make notes about these two questions:

- How interesting is the program?
- How easy is it to distinguish between the program itself and the commercials?

Now conduct the experiment yourself. A good way to record your results is to use a chart. Your chart should be similar to the one at the top of page 90.

Task 1	Task 2		Task 3
Name of program:	Name of program:		Name of program:
Technical Manipulations (Make a check mark (✔) each time the manipulation occurs.)	Images (Make a check mark (✔) each time the image occurs.) Positive Negative		Thoughts about: • Interest of program • Ease of distinguishing program from commercials
Cuts:			
Fades:			
Zooms:			
Voice-overs:			
Other:			

2 Analyze your data. If you wish, you can compare your results with McGrane's results (see the bottom of this page).

1 How many technical manipulations did you count?

2 How many positive images did you see on the news? How many negative ones? What kinds of images do you particularly remember?

3 How interesting was it to watch TV with no sound? How easy was it to distinguish between the program and the commercials?

3 Prepare a short (three- to four-minute) presentation to give to a small group about your experience. Describe:

- the TV programs you watched for each ten-minute period.
- the results of the data you gathered during each ten-minute period.

4 Discuss the following questions in your group or as a class.

1 Why do you think TV programs have so many technical manipulations?

2 Did you see more positive or more negative images on the news? Are you surprised at what you saw?

3 How did the absence of sound affect your viewing?

Results of McGrane's "The Un-TV Experiment"

Task 1: Participants found up to 180 technical manipulations in ten minutes. **Task 2:** Participants found a huge number of negative images. **Task 3:** Participants found that ten minutes of sound-free TV was boring. Many of them lost their concentration and had difficulty distinguishing between the program and the commercials.

4 ACADEMIC LISTENING AND NOTE TAKING: Dangers of the Mass Media

In this section you will hear and take notes on a two-part lecture given by Dedra Smith, a media expert who conducts workshops about media and society. The title of the lecture is *Dangers of the Mass Media*. Ms. Smith will describe what she believes are some harmful effects of the media today.

BEFORE THE LECTURE

PERSONALIZING THE TOPIC

1 Read the following information from the *New York Times 2002 Almanac*.

> A great majority of American households have two or more televisions. According to the A.C. Nielsen Company, which monitors television viewership, at least one of these televisions was on in each household for 7 hours and 37 minutes per day during the 1998–99 television season. That's 1 hour and 18 minutes more than in 1971, when the average was just over 6 hours and 19 minutes, but 3 minutes less than in 1997–98.
>
> Average daily viewing per person is still much higher than the 1970s levels, but down slightly from the year before. Women over the age of 18 watched longest: they averaged 4 hours and 51 minutes per day, while men over 18 watched for 4 hours and 16 minutes. Children aged 12–17 watched an average of 2 hours and 54 minutes.

2 For each of the forms of media in the following chart, write how many hours you spend using it per day and per week. Then compare your chart with a partner.

Media	Hours per day	Hours per week
TV		
Telephone		
Video games		
Newspapers		
Magazines		
Movies		
Internet		
Other		

3 Discuss the following questions with your partner.

1 For what purposes do you use each of the forms of media in the chart?

2 Do you think you spend too much time using any of these forms of media? Why or why not?

NOTE TAKING: ORGANIZING YOUR NOTES AS A MAP

> One way of taking notes is called *mapping*. In this method, you write the main idea on your paper and draw lines out to related points. As you take notes, you can show connections between different parts of the lecture by adding lines.

1 | Look at the following map of excerpts from Part One of Ms. Smith's lecture.

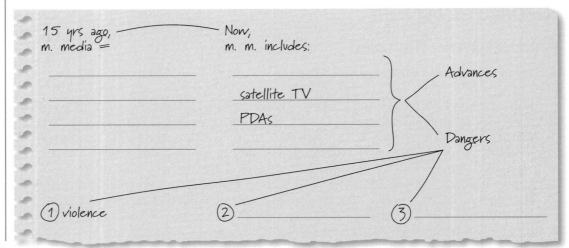

2 | Now listen to the excerpts and complete the map. ▶ **PLAY**

3 | Compare your map with a partner.

LECTURE, PART ONE: Issues of Violence, Passivity, and Addiction

GUESSING VOCABULARY FROM CONTEXT

1 | The following items contain important vocabulary from Part One of the lecture. Work with a partner. Using the context and your knowledge of related words, take turns trying to guess the meanings of the words in **bold**.

_____ **1** These new advances bring us dangers that we should be **aware of**.

_____ **2** Many people are afraid that children and adolescents are especially **susceptible** to this violence.

_____ **3** Kids set a **subway booth** on fire.

_____ **4** **Tragically**, the man working at the booth died.

_____ **5** TV can make us **passive**.

_____ **6** Using the media can become very **addictive**.

_____ **7** Most of us **wander** through cyberspace . . . wasting a lot of time.

2 Work with your partner. Match the vocabulary terms with their definitions by writing the letter of each definition below in the blank next to the sentence containing the correct term in step 1. Check your answers in a dictionary if necessary.

    a hard to stop or give up
    b office that sells metro cards or tokens
    c informed about
    d likely to be affected by
    e sadly
    f move with no clear direction or purpose
    g not wanting to do anything; inactive

NOTE TAKING: ORGANIZING YOUR NOTES AS A MAP

1 Look at the following map. It is a map for all of Part One of the lecture. Notice that you already know some of the missing information because you listened to excerpts from Part One in the note-taking task on page 92. Copy your answers from that task on to the appropriate lines in this map.

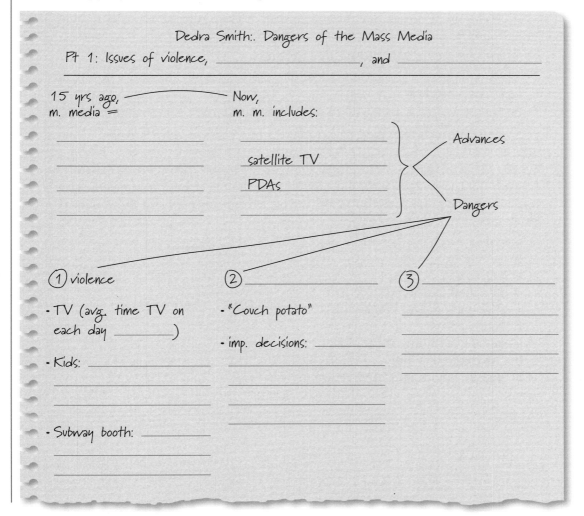

Dedra Smith:. Dangers of the Mass Media

Pt 1: Issues of violence, _____ , and _____

15 yrs ago,   Now,
m. media =   m. m. includes:

                                              Advances

                  satellite TV

                  PDAs

                                          Dangers

① violence   ② _____   ③ _____

- TV (avg. time TV on   - "Couch potato"
  each day _____)
                 - imp. decisions: _____

- Kids: _____

- Subway booth: _____

2 | Now listen to Part One of the lecture and complete the map. ▶ **PLAY**

3 | Compare your map with a partner.

LECTURE, PART TWO: Issues of Advertising and Invasion of Privacy

GUESSING VOCABULARY FROM CONTEXT

1 | The following items contain important vocabulary from Part One of the lecture. Work with a partner. Using the context and your knowledge of related words, take turns trying to guess the meanings of the words in **bold**.

_____ **1** The content is just an excuse, or a kind of **wrapping**, for the advertising.

_____ **2** There is an essential **marketing** relationship between the media, the advertiser, and the user.

_____ **3** Even **print media** has a high percentage of ads.

_____ **4** We are used to being **bombarded** by endless commercials.

_____ **5** Many of us use our remote controls to **zap out** the advertising with the mute button.

_____ **6** The media is **invading our privacy**.

_____ **7** Advertisers gather statistical data about people like you – **potential consumers**.

_____ **8** Information about you can be **compiled** and sold to other companies.

_____ **9** you can be **tracked** if you make a few visits to any Web site.

2 | Work with your partner. Match the vocabulary terms with their definitions by writing the letter of each definition below in the blank next to the sentence containing the correct term in step 1. Check your answers in a dictionary if necessary.

    a cover
    b get rid of
    c gathered
    d attacked, bothered
    e newspapers and magazines
    f followed
    g getting into our private lives
    h buying and selling
    i people who might buy something

∩ NOTE TAKING: ORGANIZING YOUR NOTES AS A MAP

1 | Look at the following notes from Part Two of the lecture. The note taker has just written down the words that he or she heard, without taking the time to organize them clearly. Think about the best way to organize this information in a map.

> 4. increase in advertising
>
>   past different, now ads everywhere (TV, mags . . .)
>
>   marketing — media ⟷ advertiser ⟷ user
>   TV — endless commercials
>   Remote no help because product placement: soft drinks, shoes, etc.
>
> 5. not just advertising but invasion of privacy
>   get info about you . . . credit cards . . . junk mail . . . address . . .
>   phone calls . . .
>
>   Internet: collect info about you . . . your habits
>   Message: having more = success
>
>   True? Are we what we buy?

2 | Now listen to the lecture and take notes on your own paper. ▶ **PLAY**

3 | Use your notes to help you make a complete map of the lecture. You can either copy the map of Part 1 on page 93 on your own paper and add to it, or make another map in your own style.

4 | Compare your map with a partner.

AFTER THE LECTURE

APPLYING WHAT YOU HAVE LEARNED

1 | Ms. Smith argues that two of the worst dangers of the mass media are its invasion of our privacy and its focus on trying to sell us something. According to research by the magazine *Advertising Age,* the average consumer is exposed to about three thousand advertising messages a day. Look at the left column on page 96. It shows a list of activities in a day in the life of an imaginary college student. Work with a partner and try to think of every situation in which the student is being targeted as a possible consumer. Write as many ideas as you can in the column on the right. Use your own paper if necessary.

Day in the life of a student	Marketing messages

6:30	Asleep
7:00	Clock radio goes off; student stays in bed
7:30	Gets up and showers
7:50	Gets dressed
8:00	Eats breakfast
8:15	Checks e-mail
8:30	Turns on TV to check weather
8:45	Looks at newspaper and then leaves house
9:00	Goes into a local shop to buy pens
9:15	Takes bus or subway to school
12:30	Eats lunch at a fast-food restaurant
1:00	Goes to library
3:30	Buys book in bookstore using a credit card
4:00	Goes to the movies with friends
7:30	Returns home, cooks dinner
9:00	Gets a phone call from a telemarketer
10:00	Goes online
11:00	Watches sports on TV
12:00	Goes to bed

Marketing messages: Student hears several commercials

2 Discuss the following questions with your partner.

1 Compare your life with the student in step 1. Do you have more advertising in your life? Less? The same?

2 Do you think that you are influenced by advertising? Why or why not?

3 Are you worried about the effects of the media? If so, what do you think is the worst effect?

Breaking the Rules

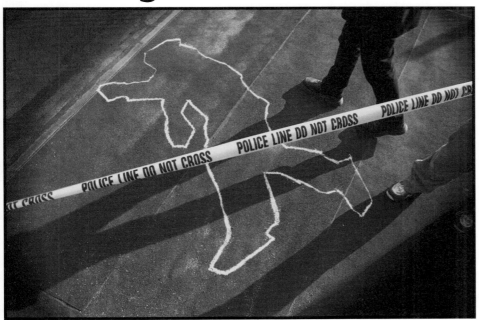

This unit examines crime and punishment. In Chapter 7, you will hear interviews with parents who are concerned about crime, and with two crime victims. You will also hear a lecture on types of crime and methods of solving crime. In Chapter 8, you will hear two perspectives on how society should try to keep crime rates low, including ways to prevent crime and punish criminals. The lecture is on one of the most controversial topics in the United States today – the death penalty.

Chapter 7

Crime and Criminals

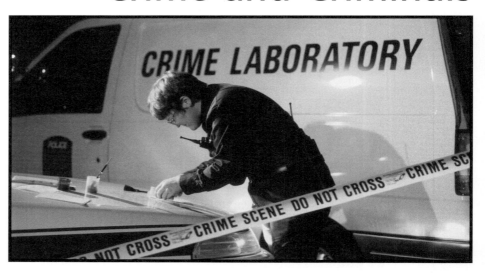

1 GETTING STARTED

In this section you are going to discuss deviance, crime, and types of crime. You will also listen to some news reports about different types of crime.

READING AND THINKING ABOUT THE TOPIC

1 | Read the following passage.

In all societies, some behaviors conform to what is expected while other behaviors are thought of as *deviant* – that is, they are viewed as unacceptable. Some deviant behavior is illegal. A *crime* is a deviant act that is prohibited by the law.

The U.S. legal system recognizes two main categories of crime. *Felonies* are serious crimes; *misdemeanors* are less serious. Crime can be violent or nonviolent. White-collar crime refers to illegal business transactions. Blue-collar crime refers to small crimes such as shoplifting and also to serious crimes such as robbery and murder. There are also "modern" crimes that have been made possible by technology, such as crimes connected with the Internet.

It is difficult to know how many crimes are committed because most crimes are not reported, and most criminals are not caught.

2 | Answer the following questions according to the information in the passage.

1 What is deviant behavior? Is deviant behavior always a crime?

2 What are two categories of crime?

3 What makes it difficult to know how many crimes are committed?

3 | Read these questions and share your answers with a partner.

1 What different types of crime do you know about?

2 How is crime punished in your community?

SHARING YOUR OPINION

1 | Work in a small group. Look at the photograph and discuss whether you think the photograph shows deviant behavior. Explain the reasons for your answers.

2 | Read the list of deviant behaviors below. Number them in order of how wrong or unacceptable they are: 1 = most unacceptable; 10 = most acceptable.

_____ Getting into the bus or subway without paying a fare

_____ Paying for one movie ticket in a multiplex theater, and then going into a second movie without paying

_____ Taking paper or office supplies from your school or workplace

_____ Receiving too much change from a cashier for a purchase and not returning it

_____ Buying counterfeit goods, such as a homemade CD

_____ Making a copy of a CD and giving it to your friends

_____ Damaging someone's parked car and not leaving your contact information

_____ Buying something that you know was stolen

_____ Keeping an item that was delivered to you by mistake

_____ Asking your doctor to help you get treatment that your insurance doesn't normally pay for

3 | Discuss with your group whether you would consider any of the behaviors in step 2 to be crimes.

BRAINSTORMING ABOUT THE TOPIC

When you brainstorm about a topic, you allow yourself to think about it freely and can generate unexpected ideas and reactions. A good way to brainstorm is to use a word map that indicates your ideas about different aspects of the topic.

1 Work with a partner. Look at the word map below. Think about crime and brainstorm different aspects of crime. You may, for example, focus on types of crime, causes and effects of crime, personal experiences with crime, punishments for crime, or any other aspects of crime that occur to you. Write notes about your thoughts on the word map. Add as many lines to the word map as you wish.

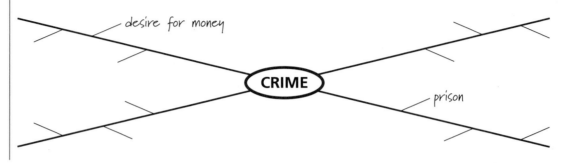

2 Share your ideas with another pair of classmates.

⌒ BUILDING BACKGROUND KNOWLEDGE ON THE TOPIC: TECHNICAL TERMS

Many fields of study have technical terms that you need to know in order to understand and discuss topics in that field.

1 Read the technical terms for various types of crime and their definitions (given in parentheses) in the left column of the chart below. Then listen to a series of radio crime reports. As you listen, write the number of the report next to the type of crime that is being reported. ▶ **PLAY**

Type of crime	Report number
Arson (setting property on fire)	
Burglary (going into a building to steal something)	
Motor vehicle theft (stealing a car)	
Murder (killing someone, also called "homicide")	
Rape (forcing someone to have sexual relations)	
Shoplifting (stealing from a store)	
Weapons possession (having a weapon without a license)	

2 Compare your answers with a partner.

2 AMERICAN VOICES: Evelina, Arpad, Gail, and Tom

In this section you will hear four people share their opinions about crime. First, you will hear Evelina and Arpad, the parents of a young boy, discuss their fears about crime in society. Then Gail, a professional dancer, and Tom, a graduate student, will talk about being crime victims.

BEFORE THE INTERVIEWS

EXAMINING GRAPHIC MATERIAL

1 | Look at the two pie charts below that classify arrests in the United States today. The chart on the left classifies arrests by age group. The chart on the right classifies arrests by gender. Work with a partner. Fill in the chart legends with your guesses about the age and gender of people arrested.

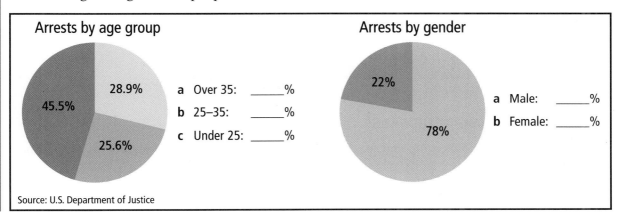

Arrests by age group

28.9%
45.5%
25.6%

a Over 35: _____%
b 25–35: _____%
c Under 25: _____%

Arrests by gender

22%
78%

a Male: _____%
b Female: _____%

Source: U.S. Department of Justice

2 | Check your responses using the answer key at the bottom of page 102. Were your guesses correct? Does any of the information surprise you?

INTERVIEW WITH EVELINA AND ARPAD: Crime in society today

Here are some words and phrases from the interview with Evelina and Arpad printed in **bold** and given in the context in which you will hear them. They are followed by definitions.

I've never actually been **struck** by crime: *personally affected*

I see big groups of kids **roaming** the streets: *walking around with no clear purpose*

if it's a **rowdy** teenage group: *noisy, wild*

Guns might not be **visible**: *able to be seen*

I've never seen anyone with a gun and **much less** seen a shooting: *even less, certainly haven't*

It's very **random**: that's what worries me: *without any definite pattern*

A **bullet** struck him in the leg: *small metal object fired from a gun*

Kids who get into **gangs** don't have that much contact with other people: *groups of young people who are involved in antisocial or illegal activities*

It's a **recipe for disaster**: *situation that will lead to serious trouble*

The government has such a **slack** attitude toward guns: *lazy, not interested*

Arpad, Daniel, and Evelina

☊ ANSWERING TRUE/FALSE QUESTIONS

1 | Read the following statements before you listen to the interview with Arpad and Evelina.

_____ **1** Evelina is concerned about the crime news that she sees on TV.

_____ **2** Arpad is not bothered by loud groups of teenagers on the street.

_____ **3** Evelina is not worried about the availability of guns.

_____ **4** Arpad says that someone was recently shot in a local restaurant.

_____ **5** Evelina says that parents need to have more contact with their children.

_____ **6** Arpad blames the high levels of crime on the availability of guns.

_____ **7** Arpad thinks that teachers have the main responsibility for teaching values to children.

_____ **8** Arpad supports gun control by the government.

2 | Listen to the interview and take notes. Use your notes to answer the questions above. Write *T* (true) or *F* (false) in the blanks. ▶ **PLAY**

3 | Compare your answers with a partner.

Answers to "Examining Graphic Material," page 101
Left chart: a Over 35 = 28.9%   **b** 25–35 = 25.6%   **c** Under 25 = 45.5%
Right chart: a Male = 78%   **b** Female = 22%

INTERVIEW WITH GAIL AND TOM: *Being the victim of a crime*

Gail often works late at night. Once she was robbed by some young men, and she explains what happened. Tom talks about being the victim of burglars and pickpockets.

Here are some words and phrases from the interview with Gail and Tom printed in **bold** and given in the context in which you will hear them. They are followed by definitions.

Once I was **mugged** by some young kids: *attacked and robbed*

You're **ruining** your lives: *destroying*

Kids like that don't need **prosecuting**: *being charged with a crime and taken to court*

Kids are so **vulnerable**: *easily influenced*

It's almost a **macho** type of thing: *strong and manly*

The apartment was **ransacked**: *broken into, searched, and left in a messy condition*

I lost **irreplaceable** personal items: *something you can never get again*

It's like a feeling of **violation**: *invasion*

I called the police so that I could have a record of what was stolen **for tax purposes**: *in order to be able to deduct the amount of the stolen property from your taxes*

I've had things taken by **pickpockets**: *thieves who steal things out of pockets or bags, especially in crowds*

It had **symbolic** value: *emotional, sentimental*

⌒ RETELLING WHAT YOU HAVE HEARD

One way to be sure that you have understood what you have heard is to be able to retell the information to someone else from memory. You do not need to use the same words that the speaker used.

1 Read the following questions before you listen to the interview with Gail and Tom.

  1 What happened to Gail? Where was she? What was stolen?

  2 What was stolen from Tom? Where and how?

  3 How did they feel about being victims of crime?

  4 Did they report the incidents?

2 Now, listen to the interview and take notes. **PLAY**

Gail

Tom

3 Work with a partner. Take turns retelling what Gail and Tom said. Be sure to include answers to all the questions in step 1. (You can review your notes first, but don't look at them while you are speaking.)

AFTER THE INTERVIEWS

EXAMINING GRAPHIC MATERIAL

1 Look at the graph below. It shows the percentage of selected crimes reported to the police.

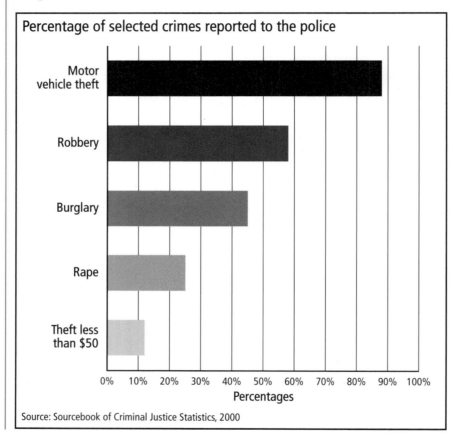

Percentage of selected crimes reported to the police

Percentages

Source: Sourcebook of Criminal Justice Statistics, 2000

2 Discuss the following questions with a partner. Base your answers on the graph in step 1 and your own ideas.

1 Which crimes get reported most frequently?

2 Which crimes are reported least frequently?

3 How do you explain the fact that people report some crimes less than others?

4 According to official statistics, it is estimated that less than half of all crimes are reported to the police. Why do you think this is true?

PERSONALIZING THE TOPIC

Imagine that you are in situations similar to those of the people who were interviewed. What would you do? Circle the letters of all the answers that apply. Compare your responses with a partner.

1 You are alone in a city and it is late. You need to get home. Would you . . .
   a take the bus or train, even if you have to wait a long time?
   b walk home quickly but without being very concerned?
   c decide not to go home, but to stay with some friends nearby?

2 If a stranger approached you, would you . . .
   a act calmly and talk to the stranger?
   b run away as fast as you could?
   c ignore the person and keep on walking?

3 If someone told you to hand over your money, would you . . .
   a agree to give the person your money?
   b say nothing and pretend not to hear?
   c refuse to give them the money?

4 If a person stole a small amount of money from you, would you . . .
   b be very hurt and afraid?
   c feel sorry for the criminal?
   d feel angry about what happened?

5 If your apartment were broken into, would you . . .
   a expect the police to help?
   b expect the police to do nothing?
   c feel very violated?

3 IN YOUR OWN VOICE

In this section you will discuss various aspects of crime and criminals. You will practice speaking about your knowledge, ideas, and values.

SHARING YOUR OPINION

1 | Look at the "game board" below. It has questions about different aspects of crime and criminals. Circulate among your classmates, using the game board to ask questions (one question per classmate). If your classmate can give you a well-developed answer to a question – not just one sentence – write the name of the classmate in that box and make some brief notes about the answer. When you complete three boxes across and three down, stop the activity.

Find someone who . . .		
has a recommendation about how to reduce the level of crime in society.	has an opinion about the causes of crime and can explain what makes someone break the law.	knows the name and story of a famous criminal in history.
has read a crime novel or seen a crime movie and can tell you the story.	can offer an explanation of the high level of violent crime in the United States.	can describe a really well-publicized crime – something that dominated the newspapers and TV and captured the public's interest.
can comment on one of the following types of crime: • youth crime • crimes committed by women • Internet crime	can describe an activity that is considered illegal but that the person believes should be legalized.	has been the victim of a crime and is prepared to tell the story of what happened.

2 | Work in small groups. Take turns explaining some of the answers you got from your classmates. Then choose the most interesting answer in your group and share it with the class.

4 ACADEMIC LISTENING AND NOTE TAKING: Crime and Ways of Solving Crime

In this section you will hear and take notes on a two-part lecture by Professor Michael Anglin, a lawyer who is interested in methods that are used to find criminals. The title of the lecture is *Crime and Ways of Solving Crime*. Professor Anglin will review categories and types of crime, and go on to discuss some methods of solving crime.

BEFORE THE LECTURE

BUILDING BACKGROUND KNOWLEDGE ON THE TOPIC: TECHNICAL TERMS

One way to begin to become familiar with the technical vocabulary of a particular subject is to try organizing it into word groups. Surprisingly, you might find that you understand more than you think you do.

Look at the word map for organizing different kinds of crime vocabulary. Then read the list of words below the word map. Work with a partner and write the words in the appropriate word groups on the map. Use a dictionary if necessary. You can also ask other classmates or your teacher for help.

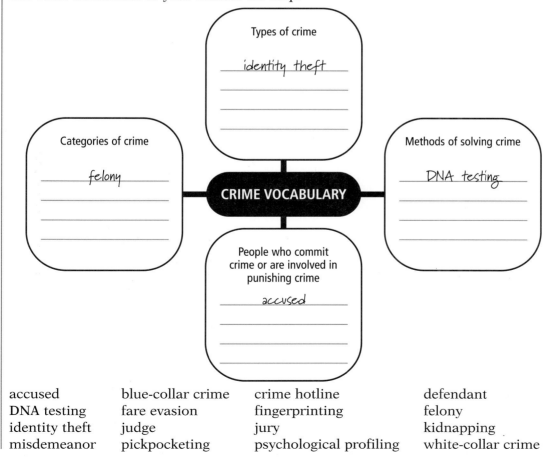

accused	blue-collar crime	crime hotline	defendant
DNA testing	fare evasion	fingerprinting	felony
identity theft	judge	jury	kidnapping
misdemeanor	pickpocketing	psychological profiling	white-collar crime

⌒ NOTE TAKING: CLARIFYING YOUR NOTES

If you find that there are some parts of a lecture that you cannot understand because the lecturer is speaking quickly or the ideas and vocabulary are difficult, do not panic!

Develop a system that you can use during a lecture for noting down ideas or words that you need to check. The fastest way is to use circles, question marks, or asterisks to mark problem items. You can use this method during the lecture itself.

After the lecture, make notes of your questions in the margin. Your questions could involve minor items, such as spelling, or major items, such as comprehension of an idea or opinion.

Take the time to clarify any information that you do not understand. Most lecturers will encourage you to ask questions. Otherwise, you can try to clarify anything that you do not understand by asking your classmates, looking in your textbook, or doing research in a library or online.

1 | Look at the student's notes below. They are notes on the beginning of Professor Anglin's lecture. The circles, question marks, and asterisks indicate things that the student has not understood. Now look at the right side of the page and notice the questions about these things that the student has written.

> Prof. Michael Anglin: Crime and Ways of Solving Crime
>
> I Crime — 2 cats
>   A. Felonies and Misdimors (sp??)   spelling?
>   B. mis =>15/50?? days & <1 yr.   15 or 50 days?
> II Legal process
>   A. Accused goes thru legal process
>   B. Goes to judge or jury
>   C. ****decides punishment   who decides: judge
>   or jury?

2 | Listen to an excerpt from the lecture and try to answer the student's questions. ▶ PLAY

3 | Ask other classmates for clarification, if necessary.

LECTURE, PART ONE: Types of Crime

GUESSING VOCABULARY FROM CONTEXT

1 | The following items contain important vocabulary from Part One of the lecture. Work with a partner. Using the context and your knowledge of related words, take turns trying to guess the meanings of the words in **bold**.

_____ **1** A misdemeanor is **broadly** defined as . . .

_____ **2** A felony carries a term of **imprisonment**.

_____ **3** Some of the more serious felonies include **robbery** . . .

_____ **4** Another way in which people may **classify** crime is . . .

_____ **5** White-collar crime includes **tax fraud**.

_____ **6** White-collar crime also includes **embezzlement**.

_____ **7** Corporate crime is committed by people of **high social status**.

_____ **8** Your **credit** will be ruined.

2 | Work with your partner. Match the vocabulary terms with their definitions by writing the letter of each definition below in the blank next to the sentence containing the correct term in step 1. Check your answers in a dictionary if necessary.

a financial reputation
b stealing money from the place where you work
c loosely, generally
d cheating on your taxes
e important position in society
f time spent in prison (jail)
g using force to steal
h organize, categorize

⌒ NOTE TAKING: CLARIFYING YOUR NOTES

1 | Listen to Part One of the lecture and take notes on your own paper. Use circles, question marks, or asterisks to signal any parts of the lecture that you do not understand. **▶ PLAY**

2 | Write your questions in the margin.

3 | Clarify your notes by finding the answers to your questions.

4 | Compare your notes with a partner.

LECTURE, PART TWO: Ways of Solving Crime

GUESSING VOCABULARY FROM CONTEXT

The following items contain important vocabulary from Part Two of the lecture. Work with a partner. Using the context and your knowledge of related words, choose the best synonym for the words in **bold** by circling the correct letters. Check your answers in a dictionary if necessary.

1 As long as there has been crime, there have been ways to **solve it**.
   a find and catch the criminals
   b prevent and record crime
   c prosecute and punish crime

2 One of the oldest methods is **interrogation**.
   a interview
   b discussion
   c questioning

3 This system allows people to give information to the police **anonymously**.
   a in person
   b without giving their names
   c using the telephone

4 In some cases, **law enforcement personnel** have difficulty finding a criminal.
   a members of the public
   b witnesses
   c members of the police

5 Each person's fingerprint is **unique**.
   a individual
   b similar
   c recognizable

6 It was only in the late nineteenth century that fingerprints were first used to **identify** criminals.
   a find the motive of
   b establish the identity of
   c locate the position of

7 There were some cases where **nannies** were accused of abusing the children they were paid to take care of.
   a friends
   b relatives
   c babysitters

8 Each person, with the exception of **identical siblings**, has a unique DNA coding system.
   a brothers and sisters
   b relatives
   c twins

🎧 NOTE TAKING: USING YOUR NOTES TO ANSWER TEST QUESTIONS

One reason for taking notes is so that you can remember what you have heard well enough to answer questions on a test or quiz. Sometimes in college classes you are given the questions you will be asked before you hear a lecture. Thinking about these questions ahead of time will help you focus on the main ideas and important details as you listen to the lecture and take notes.

1 Read the following questions before you listen to the lecture. Make sure you understand what is being asked.

1 Professor Anglin talks about interrogation as an important part of solving crimes. What is interrogation and how is it helpful?

2 A "crime hotline" is a system that the police sometimes use to find criminals. It involves asking private citizens to give information to the police by making an anonymous phone call or logging onto a website anonymously. Who is likely to use this system, and why?

3 Using fingerprints is one of the oldest ways of identifying a criminal. Why are fingerprints one of the most useful tools in crime investigations?

4 Psychological profiling is a crime-solving technique practiced by criminal psychologists. What does psychological profiling involve?

5 Hidden cameras make it possible to record all activity in the area covered by the camera. What is controversial about this form of crime detection?

6 The analysis of DNA found at the scene of a crime is a new and effective technique for solving crimes. Is it always accurate?

2 Listen to the second part of the lecture and take notes on your own paper using an organizational format of your choice. Listen carefully for the answers to the questions above. ▶ **PLAY**

3 Clarify your notes if necessary. Then work with a partner and take turns giving oral answers to the questions in step 1. Do not look at your notes while you are speaking.

AFTER THE LECTURE

APPLYING WHAT YOU HAVE LEARNED

1 Look in newspapers and magazines for an article about a crime investigation or a trial. Make notes about the following questions.

1 What happened?

2 Who was involved?

3 Where did it take place?

4 When did it take place?

2 | Review the various methods for solving crimes that Professor Anglin explained. Were any of these methods mentioned in the crime investigation or trial that you read about?

- crime hotlines
- interrogation
- fingerprinting
- psychological profiling
- hidden cameras
- DNA evidence

3 | Tell a partner about the article you read and the crime-solving methods the article mentioned.

THINKING CRITICALLY ABOUT THE TOPIC

Work in a small group. Look at the cartoon and discuss the following questions.

1 What do you think the terms *kickbacks* and *price fixing* might refer to?

2 Can you describe some white-collar crimes that happened in the past? Do you know about any that have happened recently?

3 Do you believe that white-collar crime is punished severely enough? Explain.

"KICKBACKS, EMBEZZLEMENT, PRICE-FIXING, BRIBERY... THIS IS AN EXTREMELY HIGH-CRIME AREA."

Controlling Crime

1 GETTING STARTED

In this section you are going to discuss the problem of how to control crime. Then you will listen to people express opinions about various crimes, decide how certain of their opinions the people are, and discuss whether or not you agree with them.

READING AND THINKING ABOUT THE TOPIC

1 | Read the following passage.

> Violent crime has dropped in the United States in recent years, but the overall crime rate is still alarmingly high. Crime control is one of the most difficult and controversial subjects in sociology. People have very different beliefs about the best way to lower the crime rate.
>
> Many people believe that the best way to control crime is to stop it from happening in the first place. This might mean developing educational and social programs to discourage young people from becoming involved in criminal activity, or having more

police officers on the streets. Other people think that the best way to control crime is to have tougher punishments. This might include having stricter laws, more arrests, and longer prison terms.

2 | Answer the following questions according to the information in the passage.

   1 What are two different approaches to controlling crime?

   2 How could educational and social programs help lower the crime rate?

3 | Read these questions and share your answers with a partner.

   1 Which of the two different approaches to controlling crime do you think is more effective? Why?

   2 Do you think your community has a high crime rate or a low crime rate? Explain.

🎧 LISTENING FOR OPINIONS

When people are discussing ideas, particularly if they are complex or controversial, you often have to listen closely to understand their opinions. You can hear how strongly a person feels about a topic by listening to the speaker's words and the degree of certainty with which the words are spoken. Look at the following examples:

The speaker gives an opinion.	*I think . . .* *I believe . . .* *I feel that . . .* *In my opinion . . .*
The speaker is very sure of his or her opinion.	*I really think . . .* *I really believe . . .* *I am convinced that . . .* *I am certain that . . .* *That's an excellent idea!* *That's terrible!* *That's awful!*
The speaker is not really sure of his or her opinion.	*Mmm . . . well . . . let me see . . .* *Well . . . maybe . . .* *I don't know . . .* *I guess . . .* *I'm not really sure, but . . .*

1 | Read the technical terms and definitions for various types of crime in the left column of the chart on page 115. Read the examples of each type of crime in the right column.

Type of crime	Example
1 Assault and robbery (attacking someone and stealing their possessions)	A group of teenagers between the ages of 15 and 17 attack an old man as he walks home. They steal his wallet and beat him with a baseball bat, leaving him unconscious on the sidewalk.
2 Abduction (taking a person against his or her will)	A woman who is divorced from her husband secretly takes the couple's 13-year-old son and runs off with him to another country. The father and mother share custody of the son.
3 Vandalism (destroying property)	Some teenagers break into a school cafeteria and smash all the plates. Then they spray paint the walls.
4 Delinquent payment (not paying money that you owe)	A couple who are renting an apartment have not paid their rent for the last three months.
5 Impersonation / Breaking and entering (pretending to be someone else and entering somewhere illegally)	A man knocks on the door of an elderly woman's house, pretending to be a TV repairman. Once inside, he asks to use the bathroom, but, instead, he goes into the bedroom and steals money and jewelry.
6 False ID (having identification papers that identify you as someone else)	An 18-year-old makes a copy of his friend's college ID. He uses it to pretend that he is 21.

2 Listen to people express their opinions about the crimes in step 1. Listen carefully to what they say and the degree of certainty with which they express their opinions. Circle the degree of certainty that the speaker expresses. ▶ **PLAY**

1   Sure   Not sure

2   Sure   Not sure

3   Sure   Not sure

4   Sure   Not sure

5   Sure   Not sure

6   Sure   Not sure

3 Compare your answers with a partner. Then tell your partner about any of the cases where you disagree with the people you heard.

2 AMERICAN VOICES: David and Amy

In this section you will hear David, a young man who works with high school students before they go to college, talk about the importance of preventing juvenile crime. Then Amy will give a lawyer's perspective on crime control.

BEFORE THE INTERVIEWS

SHARING YOUR OPINION

1 | What is your opinion about controlling crime? Write *A* (agree) or *D* (disagree) next to the following opinions.

_____ 1 Criminals should be punished. If people break the law, they deserve to pay the price, no matter why they did it.

_____ 2 Having tough punishments can stop people from committing crimes. If we have severe punishments, people will think twice before they break the law.

_____ 3 People need a second chance. If we try to reform criminals, by education, psychological treatment, or other methods, we can turn them away from a life of crime.

_____ 4 We need to provide a sense of security in society. Putting people who break the law in prison is the only way to do that.

_____ 5 The most important thing we can do is try to prevent crime before it happens. Prevention is always better than punishment.

2 | Share your answers in a small group. Then discuss as a class which opinions were the most controversial.

INTERVIEW WITH DAVID: Preventing juvenile crime

Here are some words and phrases from the interview with David printed in **bold** and given in the context in which you will hear them. They are followed by definitions.

I think the media **exacerbates** the problem: *makes worse*

We have thousands of security guards in the schools and **metal detectors**, too: *machines that can detect guns, knives, and other weapons made of metal*

And the kids get **searched** as they go into school: *physically examined to see if they have weapons or illegal drugs*

They are more likely to **lash out** and become violent: *express anger*

Put them on a **one-to-one basis** and they're usually very friendly: *with one other person*

The problem is that **social support systems** have really **fallen apart**: *government and private organizations that give people help and encouragement / become worse due to lack of money*

The **funding** for programs like these has been cut: *money*

But we also need **harsher** punishments: *stronger, more serious*

Drug crimes carry a maximum **sentence** of twenty years or life imprisonment: *punishment*

🎧 LISTENING FOR SPECIFIC INFORMATION

1 Read the following questions before you listen to the interview with David.

   1 What does David think causes young people to commit crimes?

   2 How do kids feel about school? Why?

   3 Does David believe that violent kids are products of their social environment, or that they have natural, biological tendencies to be that way?

   4 What kinds of programs does David think schools should organize?

   5 Does David believe in harsh punishments?

David

2 Now listen to the interview. Take notes about the answers to the questions in step 1. ▶ **PLAY**

3 Work with a partner. Take turns telling each other your answers. (You can review your notes first, but don't look at them while you are speaking.) Then share your answers as a class.

INTERVIEW WITH AMY: The prison experience

Here are some words and phrases from the interview with Amy printed in **bold** and given in the context in which you will hear them. They are followed by definitions.

what really works – not for hardened criminals, but for **first-time offenders**: *people who commit a crime for the first time*

The first step is **deterrence**: *stopping people from committing crime*

Criminals are not being **rehabilitated**: *taught how to have a socially acceptable way of life*

You end up having a lot of people in prisons who are not the **kingpins** of drug deals: *most important people*

There need to be programs that have a psychological and an educational **component**: *part*

We need to make prison a less **repressive** experience: *cruel and severe*

We need **bridge programs**: *programs that help released prisoners adjust to society*

Most criminals are **recidivists**: *repeat criminals*

so that society doesn't look at released prisoners in such a **disdainful** way: *disrespectful, critical*

so that no **stigma** is attached: *shame*

Amy

🎧 LISTENING FOR MAIN IDEAS

1 Amy does not believe that the current prison system is very effective. She describes the experience of a person before being convicted of a crime, while in prison, and after being released. Listen to the interview with Amy and fill in the chart with the main ideas that she discusses. ▶ **PLAY**

	What Amy thinks should happen	**The present situation**
Before a person is convicted of a crime and sent to prison	There should be more jobs and more social support systems.	The economy and the social structure don't help prevent crime.
While a convicted criminal is in prison		
After a person is released from prison		

2 Compare your answers with a partner.

AFTER THE INTERVIEWS

PARAPHRASING WHAT YOU HAVE HEARD

1 Following is a paraphrase of the interviews with David and Amy. Fill in the blanks using your own words. In some cases, you will need to write more than one word.

> David says that the _____ and the _____
> exacerbate the problem of juvenile crime. He believes that kids are essentially
> _____. He thinks they need more _____
> _____ systems and after-school activities. He also thinks

they need good role models. However, he believes that if someone does commit a crime, the punishment should be _____, but

_____.

Amy says that to deter people from committing crime, you have to talk about social factors such as whether there are enough _____ for everyone and enough social support systems. But if convicted criminals are sent to jail, we need programs to _____ them, such as drug treatment programs and _____ programs. Unfortunately, many of the programs that she thinks are needed have been

_____.

Amy believes that one reason there are so many recidivists is because criminals have a bad experience in jail. When prisoners are released, Amy thinks they need _____ to help them go back into society.

2 | Compare your answers with a partner. Remember that your answers will probably not be exactly the same.

EXAMINING GRAPHIC MATERIAL

1 | Look at the following bar graph. It shows the incarceration rate per 100,000 people in eight countries. *Incarceration* means being put into prison.

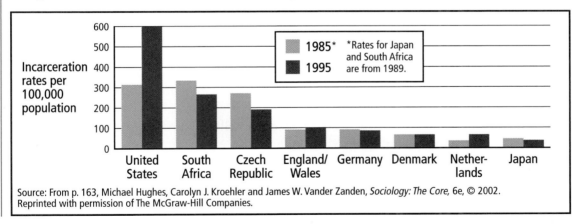

Source: From p. 163, Michael Hughes, Carolyn J. Kroehler and James W. Vander Zanden, *Sociology: The Core*, 6e, © 2002. Reprinted with permission of The McGraw-Hill Companies.

2 | Discuss the following questions with a partner.

1 Which country had the most people in prison in 1985 (or 1989)? Which country had the least people in prison?

2 Which country had the most people in prison in 1995? Which country had the least people in prison?

3 What is your reaction to the information in the graph? Does any of the information surprise you? If so, why?

4 How do you think David and Amy would react to the information in the graph?

3 IN YOUR OWN VOICE

SUPPORTING YOUR OPINION

If you are able to support your opinion, your audience will respect you because you are showing them that you have thought about the topic in depth and can develop your argument.

Support for your ideas consists of explanations and examples. You should have at least two or three pieces of supporting information. You can introduce and link your supporting information with transitional phrases, such as these:

- *first / first of all / first and foremost / to begin with*
- *in addition / additionally / secondly / furthermore / moreover / also / then / as well as*
- *finally / last but not least*

1 In the interviews, both David and Amy support their viewpoints. Look at the summaries of their arguments below. For each summary, underline the main idea, circle each piece of supporting information, and highlight linking words.

1 David believes that in order to control juvenile crime, we should try to prevent it from happening. He says that to begin with, we should have more structured after-school activities for young people. We should also have Big Brother/Big Sister programs. Additionally, we need better social support systems. And, finally, we should have harsher punishments for crimes because these would act as deterrents.

2 Amy believes that it is important to try to deter potential criminals from committing crimes. But her main point is that we should have rehabilitation procedures for criminals. First of all, there should be more programs to rehabilitate convicted criminals when they are in prison. Furthermore, these programs should have a psychological as well as an educational component. Last but not least, there should be bridge programs to help released criminals enter productive, crime-free lives.

2 Read the statements below. Then choose one with which you either agree or disagree. Support your ideas with explanations and examples.

- Some people are born with more aggressive tendencies than others.
- White-collar crime is more serious than blue-collar crime.
- Men are more likely to commit crime than women.
- Violence on TV leads to violence in society.
- The main reason for juvenile crime today is the decline of the traditional family.
- Crime is the most serious problem in society today.

3 Explain your opinion to a small group, using transitional phrases to link your supporting information. Be prepared to answer questions about what you have said.

4 As a class, discuss the ideas and make a master list of the supporting details you gathered for each argument.

4 ACADEMIC LISTENING AND NOTE TAKING: The Death Penalty

In this section you will hear and take notes on a two-part lecture given by Jonathan Stack, a filmmaker who has made several documentaries on prisons. Mr. Stack frequently lectures on criminal justice. The title of this lecture is *The Death Penalty*.

BEFORE THE LECTURE

EXAMINING GRAPHIC MATERIAL

1 | Look at the graph below. It shows the number of prisoners executed (put to death) in the United States between 1930 and 2000.

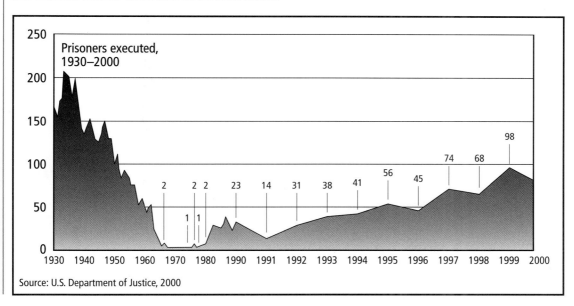

Prisoners executed, 1930–2000

Source: U.S. Department of Justice, 2000

2 | Discuss the following questions with a partner.
   1 What does the graph show about the death penalty in the United States?
   2 What is your reaction to the information in the graph?

🎧 NOTE TAKING: RECORDING NUMERICAL INFORMATION

Lecturers often present numerical information when they refer to research studies and other examples that support their ideas. It is important to listen to the context of the numerical information so that you understand what the number represents. Here are some examples of what numbers can represent:
- a year (examples: 1983, 1832)
- a percentage (examples: twenty percent, forty-four percent)
- a fraction (examples: one-eighth, three-quarters)

1 | Read the following descriptions. Each of them refers to numerical information that you will hear in the lecture.

_____ **1** The date the U.S. Supreme Court ruled that capital punishment was unconstitutional (*Capital punishment* is another term for the death penalty.)

_____ **2** The date when capital punishment was reinstated

_____ **3** The number of executions that have been carried out since capital punishment was reinstated

_____ **4** The percentage of people in the United States who say they favor the death penalty in cases of murder

_____ **5** The people in the United States who say they favor the death penalty in cases of murder, expressed as a fraction

_____ **6** The number of murders per 100,000 people per year in the United States

_____ **7** The number of murders per 100,000 people per year in Japan

_____ **8** The number of murders per 100,000 people per year in France

2 | Now listen to excerpts from the lecture. Write the correct numbers in the blanks in step 1. Then compare your answers with a partner. ▶ **PLAY**

LECTURE, PART ONE: Arguments Against the Death Penalty

GUESSING VOCABULARY FROM CONTEXT

The following items contain important vocabulary from Part One of the lecture. Work with a partner. Using the context and your knowledge of related words, choose the best synonym for the words in **bold** by circling the correct letters. Check your answers in a dictionary, if necessary.

1 The U.S. Supreme Court ruled that capital punishment was **unconstitutional**.
  a illegal   **b** immoral   **c** impossible

2 But later, the Court **reinstated** it.
  a continued to discuss it   **b** put it back in place   **c** repeated its argument

3 Executions are usually carried out by **lethal** injection or electrocution.
  a cruel   **b** deadly   **c** painless

4 States with the most executions are also the states with the highest **homicide** rates.
  a assault   **b** fraud   **c** murder

5 I have another major **objection to** capital punishment.
  a interest in   **b** criticism of   **c** opinion about

6 They were released because they were **improperly** convicted.
  a immediately   **b** angrily   **c** incorrectly

7 There were 26 people **on death row**, and 13 of them were released.
   a waiting to go to court   **b** waiting to be freed   **c** waiting for execution

8 That should not be in the **domain** of the state.
   a interest   **b** world   **c** power

⌾ NOTE TAKING: USING YOUR NOTES TO ASK QUESTIONS AND MAKE COMMENTS

Many professors in English-speaking countries expect you to ask questions and make comments during or after their lectures. In this way, information can be clarified and a variety of opinions can be introduced that increase the depth of the discussion and make it more interesting.

In Chapter 7, you practiced writing questions in the margins to remind you to clarify information that you did not understand. You can also use the margins to write comments that you would like to make. Here are some reasons you might want to ask a question or make a comment:

- You did not understand something the speaker said and want clarification.
- You would like additional information about some point of the lecture.
- You want to contribute additional information about a point of the lecture.
- You disagree with something the speaker said and want to discuss it.
- You agree with something the speaker said and want to express your support.

Even if you do not have a question or comment, it is a good idea to take notes on questions and comments of other students. You should also take notes on the lecturer's response and any class discussion that follows. This will increase your knowledge and understanding of the topic.

1 | Listen to Part One of the lecture and take notes on your own paper. ▶ **PLAY**

2 | Write your questions and comments in the margins of the paper on which you take notes. Write at least one question and one comment.

3 | Discuss your questions and comments with a partner.

LECTURE, PART TWO: Questions, answers, and comments

GUESSING VOCABULARY FROM CONTEXT

1 | The following items contain important vocabulary from Part Two of the lecture. Work with a partner. Using the context and your knowledge of related words, take turns trying to guess the meanings of the words in **bold**.

_____ 1 People's **moods** and opinions are difficult to understand through statistics.

_____ 2 This **figure** might reflect people's concern about violent crime.

_____ 3 If you've suffered the loss of a loved one, your immediate response is to want **revenge**.

_____ 4 This form of **retribution** is not the answer.

_____ 5 The legal system is supposed to **elevate us**: it is set up so that it is better than us.

_____ 6 Individually, we are **flawed**, but as a society we are strong.

_____ 7 In many ways, capital punishment is very **arbitrary**.

_____ 8 If you really believed in the death penalty as a punishment for a **horrific** crime . . .

_____ 9 Nobody would **stand for** that.

2 | Work with your partner. Match the vocabulary terms with their definitions by writing the letter of each definition below in the blank next to the sentence containing the correct term in step 1. Check your answers in a dictionary if necessary.

   a punishment for the person who hurt you
   b terrible
   c number
   d not perfect
   e unfair
   f punishment
   g help us become better
   h accept, allow
   i feelings

⌒ NOTE TAKING: USING YOUR NOTES TO ASK QUESTIONS AND MAKE COMMENTS

1 | Listen to Part Two of the lecture. You will hear five students address Mr. Stack. Take notes on their questions and comments and on Mr. Stack's responses. ▶ PLAY

2 | Compare your notes with your partner from Part One of the lecture. Were the questions and comments the students addressed to Mr. Stack similar to or different from yours?

AFTER THE LECTURE

SUMMARIZING WHAT YOU HAVE HEARD

Remember that a summary should explain the main points of a lecture in your own words.

1 Using your notes, complete the following summary of the lecture. You will need to use more than one word in most of the blanks.

The Death Penalty
Mr. Jonathan Stack

Mr. Stack said that the death penalty is the most _____ issue in criminal justice. He does not believe in capital punishment. His first argument was that capital punishment does not _____ crime. Some states that practice this form of punishment also have high rates of _____. Secondly, he argued that capital punishment is not fair. The majority of people sentenced to death are _____. Furthermore, a higher percentage of _____ are likely to be executed than whites. Finally, he pointed out that because we are human, we sometimes _____. He gave an example from the state of Illinois, where _____ _____. He concluded by arguing that killing someone is _____ _____.

   Five students responded to Stack. One of them pointed out that most Americans favor the death penalty in cases of murder. Stack explained that in his view, that opinion reflected _____ _____. Another student said that if people committed bad crimes, they deserved _____. Stack responded that the desire for revenge was a natural emotion but that laws were designed to _____ _____. He also said that if the death penalty were applied equally to all criminals, there would be about _____ a year, and that would be absurd.

---

2 Compare your summary with a partner. Remember that the ideas should be similar, but the words you use do not have to be exactly the same.

THINKING CRITICALLY ABOUT THE TOPIC

1 | Work in a small group. Look at the graph below and answer the following questions.

   1 According to the police chiefs, what is the most effective way to reduce violent crime? What is the least effective?

   2 Do you agree with the police chiefs? Why or why not?

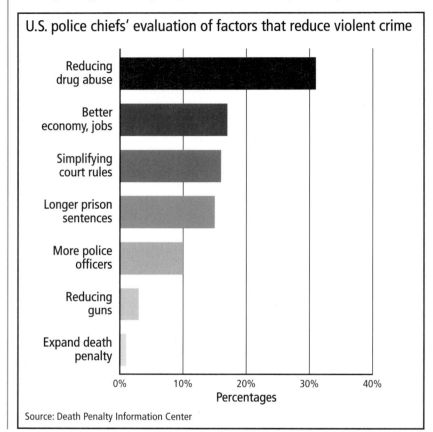

U.S. police chiefs' evaluation of factors that reduce violent crime

Reducing drug abuse
Better economy, jobs
Simplifying court rules
Longer prison sentences
More police officers
Reducing guns
Expand death penalty

0%   10%   20%   30%   40%
Percentages

Source: Death Penalty Information Center

2 | Discuss the following questions in your group.

   1 Which argument for or against the death penalty that was presented in the lecture seems the strongest to you?

   2 Can you think of any arguments for or against the death penalty that were not presented in the lecture?

Changing Societies

This unit concerns ways in which contemporary life is different from life in the past. Chapter 9 examines the impact of technology. You will hear two people with different views talk about how computers and the Internet have changed our world. The lecture is about how technology has impacted the job market. Chapter 10 presents information about the increasing tendency of people to move to cities. You will listen to interviews about the advantages and disadvantages of living in cities, near cities, and in the country. Then you will hear a lecture about how cities have changed and will continue to change.

Chapter 9

Cultural Change

1 GETTING STARTED

In this section you are going to discuss the changes in our world that are occurring because of the rapid introduction of new technology. You will also hear a mini-history of the computer and practice listening for dates.

READING AND THINKING ABOUT THE TOPIC

1 Read the following passage.

Today's world is changing faster than ever before. We have seen technological progress in areas we could not have imagined only ten or twenty years ago. Using computerized robots, a surgeon is now able to perform an operation on a patient in a different continent; music lovers can download their favorite music at the touch of a button and then burn their own CDs at home; digital photography allows us to take photographs and transmit them instantly to the other side of the world.

What is the impact of all this technology on the way we interact with each other? Nobody is quite sure yet. Some people have embraced and celebrated new technology, which allows them to save time and effort. Others are not sure if the supposed benefits are actually worth it. They are concerned that new technologies have too much importance in our lives. They believe that some new technologies are having a negative effect on the way people interact with each other.

2 Answer the following questions according to the information in the passage.

1 What are some recent innovations in the world of technology?

2 Why are some people in favor of technology?

3 Why are other people concerned about technology's impact?

3 Read these questions and share your answers with a partner.

1 In what ways has new technology improved your relationships with other people?

2 What is the most difficult experience you have had with new technology?

3 What technological innovations do you think will occur in the next fifty years?

⋒ RECORDING NUMERICAL INFORMATION

1 Look at the mini-history of the computer below. Work with a partner. Using your own ideas and knowledge, guess in which year each of the technological innovations in items 2 through 10 was made. Write your guesses in the "Guess" column.

Mini-history of the Computer

	Guess	Fact
1 In 500 B.C. the abacus, a tool for counting, was in common use.		
2 Blaise Pascal invented the first calculating machine.	_____	_____
3 The first computing machine was built that used a binary – not decimal – method of operation.	_____	_____
4 The term "artificial intelligence" was first used.	_____	_____
5 The first commercial computer with a monitor and a keyboard was developed.	_____	_____
6 The mouse was invented as a time-saving device for giving commands to a computer.	_____	_____
7 The first personal computer was marketed.	_____	_____
8 The laptop computer appeared.	_____	_____
9 "Deep Blue," a supercomputer, beat the world chess champion in a six-game match.	_____	_____
10 The first teraflop computer was installed in a laboratory. It could perform one trillion operations per second.	_____	_____

2 Listen to the mini-history of the computer. Fill in the dates that you hear in the "Fact" column. Then compare your answers with your partner. ▶ **PLAY**

2 AMERICAN VOICES: Nina and Kelly

In this section you will hear two people discuss how technology has changed the way we interact with other people. Nina, a social worker, is unsure about the benefits of computers and the Internet. Kelly, a university student, is more positive about them.

BEFORE THE INTERVIEWS

BUILDING BACKGROUND KNOWLEDGE ON THE TOPIC

Remember that it is always useful to learn something about a topic if you are going to attend a lecture on that topic. Ways to get background knowledge include

- speaking to people who have personal or professional knowledge about the topic
- doing research in a library or online
- reading novels, short stories, or poetry about the topic
- seeing a movie about the topic

1 Read the following poem, "Technology," by Angeline A. Moscatt.

> Technology gave birth to electricity
> And illuminated the night skies
> But dimmed the shining stars.
>
> Technology brought forth the telephone
> Connecting us to loved ones far away
> But cell-phone users babble* on
> Ignoring the world around them.
>
> Technology advanced step by step
> Crossbow** to gunpowder to atomic bomb
> That bomb, they say, ended a war –
> And the lives of millions of civilians.
>
> Technology – blessing or curse?
>
> *talk continuously in an excited way
> without saying anything important
> **old-fashioned weapon

2 Moscatt asks whether technology is a blessing or a curse. Work with a partner and discuss the meaning of these two words. If you are not sure, look them up in a dictionary or ask other classmates.

3 With your partner, take turns paraphrasing what Moscatt says about the three examples of technology presented in the poem:
1 electricity
2 telephones
3 weapons

INTERVIEW WITH NINA: Concerns about computers and the Internet

Here are some words and phrases from the interview with Nina, printed in **bold** and given in the context in which you will hear them. They are followed by definitions.

The amount of information is absolutely **overwhelming**: *extreme, too much to understand*

It's wonderful to have the Internet **at your disposal**: *available to use*

an electronic protector that is **incompatible with** our system: *doesn't work with*

They shut down for no **apparent** reason: *obvious*

You **toss out** some news: *send out*

Computers were **touted** as a way toward the paperless society: *praised, promoted*

It was just **misrepresented**: *described inaccurately*

Kids . . . **take it for granted**: *accept it without any questions, without thinking about it*

They learn it when they're young, and they're not **intimidated**: *frightened, scared*

🎧 LISTENING FOR OPINIONS

When discussing ideas, speakers often need to present different sides of an argument. To do this effectively, they use transitional phrases to distinguish between various viewpoints. To compare different sides of an issue, a speaker might use phrases like this:

. . . but I think . . .
. . . but other people . . .
. . . but the other thing is . . .
. . . on the other hand . . .
. . . however, some people . . .

It is important to pay attention to transitional phrases so that you understand both sides of the argument as well as the opinion of the speaker.

Nina

1 | Before you listen to the interview with Nina, read these incomplete excerpts. Notice that at the end of each one, Nina indicates that she is going to present another side of the issue. Think about what she might say.

1 It's fun to spend hours a day surfing the net, investigating something that interests you, but . . .

2 It's wonderful on one hand to have the Internet at your disposal, but . . .

3 You get to discuss books with your friends, to share the ideas with others, but . . .

4 I know a little bit about the Internet, but . . .

5 I really like e-mail, but . . .

6 Computers might be great for writing and editing things, and everything looks great and all that, but . . .

2 | Listen to Nina describe her feelings about computers and the Internet. As you listen, take notes about the opinions she expresses after each of the excerpts in step 1. Then compare your answers with a partner. ▶ **PLAY**

INTERVIEW WITH KELLY: The benefits of computers and the Internet

Here are some words and phrases from the interview with Kelly printed in **bold** and given in the context in which you will hear them. They are followed by definitions.

Letters make better **keepsakes**: *small objects that you keep because they remind you of someone or some event*

E-mail is just so much **more convenient**: *easier*

for **more extended interaction**: *longer conversations*

I have IM (Instant Messaging) **configured**: *set up on a computer*

once your get over your **initial** fear: *first, preliminary*

just **fiddling around with them** and testing things out: *using them to learn what they are like*

My generation is **hooked on** the Internet: *addicted to*

It makes a lot of things **accessible**: *available*

All of my **syllabi** for my classes are online: *plural of "syllabus" (Latin)*

The Internet could increase the **disparities** between different **classes**: *differences / levels of society*

Or maybe technology just **illuminates** existing disparities: *highlights, points out*

🎧 ANSWERING TRUE/FALSE QUESTIONS

1 | Read the following statements about Kelly's interview.

_____ **1** Compared with other people her age, Kelly is extremely good with computers.

_____ **2** Kelly thinks that the majority of adults are less comfortable with technology than she is.

_____ **3** Kelly agrees with Nina's point that letters make better keepsakes than e-mails.

_____ **4** Kelly thinks that e-mail is really good for extended interaction.

_____ **5** She checks her e-mail at least five times a day.

_____ **6** Kelly admits that chatting to your friends online is a waste of time.

_____ **7** Kelly thinks that it is possible to overcome your fear of computers.

_____ **8** Kelly believes that people who don't have computer skills will be at a disadvantage.

Kelly

2 | Listen to Kelly's interview and, for each statement in step 1, write *T* (true) or *F* (false). ▶PLAY

3 | Compare your answers with a partner.

AFTER THE INTERVIEWS

EXAMINING GRAPHIC MATERIAL

1 | Look at the graph below that shows computer ownership and Internet access in U.S. households in 1998 and 2000. In a small group, take turns describing what you see. Here are some phrases you can use:

- *Compared with (group A), (group B) . . .*
- *Between (year) and (year), (group A)'s ownership of computers increased more than (group B)'s, (group C)'s, and (group D)'s.*
- *On average, (group A) owns (far) more / fewer computers than (group B).*
- *Internet access is lower / higher among (group A) than among (group B), (group C), and (group D).*

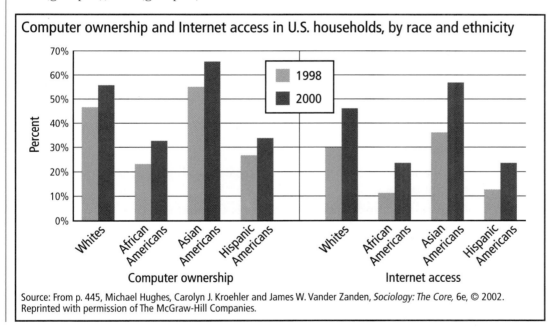

Computer ownership and Internet access in U.S. households, by race and ethnicity

Source: From p. 445, Michael Hughes, Carolyn J. Kroehler and James W. Vander Zanden, *Sociology: The Core,* 6e, © 2002. Reprinted with permission of The McGraw-Hill Companies.

2 | Read the following statements and write *A* (agree) or *D* (disagree).

_____ **1** The Internet gives you information, and information gives you power. Therefore, people without computers are at a big disadvantage.

_____ **2** On the Internet, nobody knows your race, ethnicity, gender, or age unless you want them to. Therefore, the Internet can allow more equality among people.

3 | Discuss the reasons for your answers to step 2 with your group.

3 IN YOUR OWN VOICE

In this section you will discuss a form of writing that some people, especially teenagers, are using today in their e-mails and instant messages. Then you will make a list of the rules of correct Internet behavior, or *netiquette*.

SHARING YOUR OPINION

1 | Read the following instant messages written by two high school students. Sid is in a classroom. He is writing to Charlene, who is in another class. With a partner, try to translate the message into standard English. What is Sid complaining about? What is Charlene's reaction? (Check your answers at the bottom of page 135.)

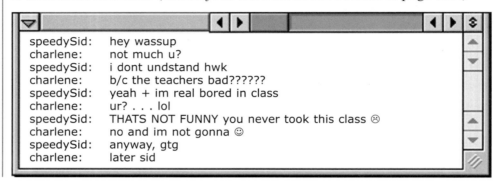

```
speedySid:    hey wassup
charlene:     not much u?
speedySid:    i dont undstand hwk
charlene:     b/c the teachers bad??????
speedySid:    yeah + im real bored in class
charlene:     ur? . . . lol
speedySid:    THATS NOT FUNNY you never took this class ☹
charlene:     no and im not gonna ☺
speedySid:    anyway, gtg
charlene:     later sid
```

2 | What is your opinion about e-mail and instant messages? Write *A* (agree) or *D* (disagree) next to the following statements. Then explain the reasons for your answers to a partner.

_____ 1 E-mail and instant messages are more efficient than telephoning or writing letters.

_____ 2 E-mail and instant messages encourage meaningful communication between people.

_____ 3 Writing e-mail and instant messages is fun and creative.

_____ 4 The rules of good writing do not apply to e-mails and instant messages.

_____ 5 E-mail and instant messages encourage people to develop bad writing habits.

3 | As a class, decide on the "do's and don'ts" of netiquette. For example, are the following behaviors acceptable or unacceptable?

- Using acronyms, such as gtg or lol
- Using emoticons, like ☹ or ☺
- Writing in capital letters
- Not using any capital letters
- Not using punctuation
- E-mailing just to say "hello"
- E-mailing jokes to all your friends
- Not including a subject line in e-mails

What are other Internet habits? Make a master list of the "do's and don'ts."

ACADEMIC LISTENING AND NOTE TAKING: Basic Work Skills Necessary in the Twenty-first Century

In this section you will hear and take notes on a two-part lecture given by Graciano E. Matos, who works in a career counseling office at a college. In his lecture, entitled *Basic Work Skills Necessary in the Twenty-first Century,* he will explain how technology has impacted office jobs.

BEFORE THE LECTURE

PERSONALIZING THE TOPIC

In his lecture, Graciano E. Matos compares old and new ways to get jobs and discusses the computer skills necessary for work in modern offices.

1 | Read the following list of computer skills. Use the list to give a grade to yourself and an older or younger family member or friend.

A = excellent; B = good; C = average; D = very weak; F = failing

	You	Older or Younger Relative or Friend
Using e-mail	_____	_____
Learning to use new software	_____	_____
Understanding hardware problems	_____	_____
Creating documents in Microsoft Word	_____	_____
Doing research online	_____	_____
Using spreadsheets	_____	_____
Creating Microsoft PowerPoint presentations	_____	_____
Making business cards and flyers	_____	_____
Creating and organizing databases	_____	_____

2 | Whose grades were generally higher – yours or those of your relative or friend? Why?

3 | Discuss the questions below with a partner. Then share your answers with the class.
   1 How do computers currently help you in your studies or in your profession?
   2 How do you think you can improve your computer skills?
   3 How do you think the Internet can help you look for a job?

SpeedySid: Hey, what's up?
Charlene: Not much. You?
SpeedySid: I don't understand the homework.
Charlene: Because the teacher's bad?
SpeedySid: Yeah, and I'm real bored in class.
Charlene: You are? (laugh out loud)
SpeedySid: That's not funny! You never took this class. ☹
Charlene: No, and I'm not going to. ☺
SpeedySid: Anyway, got to go.
Charlene: Later, Sid.

Answers to "Sharing Your Opinion," step 1, page 134

🎧 NOTE TAKING: LISTENING FOR STRESS AND INTONATION

It is important to learn to pay attention to a speaker's stress and intonation because they are a central part of the speaker's message. There are several basic patterns in spoken English that you need to be familiar with.

1 A loud or emphasized word can indicate the importance of one particular idea. It can also show contrast between two ideas:

The SECRET to preparing yourself for the working world today is . . .
In the PAST, these skills were not necessary, but NOWADAYS, they are.

2 A rising tone often indicates that the speaker is asking a question.

Did you check your résumé before you sent it?

3 A falling tone indicates that the speaker is making a statement or has completed a list.

You have to be prepared for today's workplace.

You need to be able to type fast, do research online, and

prepare PowerPoint presentations.

---

1 │ Work with a partner. Take turns reading the following sentences aloud. Predict how the speaker might use stress and intonation to draw attention to what he is saying.

- Circle the words you think the speaker will stress.
- Draw arrows to show rising or falling intonation.

1 Well, what are the skills that you need?

2 Then you decided where you were going to apply, put your résumé with a cover letter in a stamped envelope, and waited anxiously for someone to get back to you.

3 In fact, technology has not so much changed the process as enhanced it.

4 You can research employment not just in your city, but also in your state, your region, your country, and even other countries.

5 In addition to using newspapers and the phone, the Internet has become the tool of preference for getting more details on job openings, applications, and other necessary information.

2 │ Now listen to these sentences. Check to see if your predictions were accurate. Correct the circles and arrows you drew if necessary. ▶ **PLAY**

3 │ Compare what you heard with your partner.

LECTURE, PART ONE: Looking for and Applying for a Job

GUESSING VOCABULARY FROM CONTEXT

1 The following items contain important vocabulary from Part One of the lecture. Work with a partner. Using the context and your knowledge of related words, take turns trying to guess the meanings of the words in **bold**.

_____ **1** making phone calls to **prospective** employers

_____ **2** put your résumé with a **cover letter** in a stamped envelope . . .

_____ **3** The tools used are much more advanced, and they require more skills and **expertise**.

_____ **4** Technology has not so much changed the process as **enhanced** it.

_____ **5** This makes the **search** more open.

_____ **6** people of different **socioeconomic** backgrounds from all over the world

_____ **7** The Internet has become the **tool of preference** for getting more details.

_____ **8** You might have had a desk full of newspaper ads just to **keep track of** where you should apply.

2 Work with your partner. Match the vocabulary terms with their definitions by writing the letter of each definition below in the blank next to the sentence or phrase containing the correct term in step 1. Check your answers in a dictionary if necessary.

a possible
b a letter to explain what you are sending
c improved
d organize and remember
e social and financial status in society
f attempt to find something
g ability
h favorite way

🎧 NOTE TAKING: LISTENING FOR STRESS AND INTONATION

The stress and intonation patterns that a lecturer uses can help you to understand the lecture. Review the patterns described in "Note Taking: Listening for Stress and Intonation," on page 136. As you begin to notice these patterns, you will find that they can help you understand the structure of a lecture and its important points. This will make it easier for you to take good notes.

1 Now listen to Part One of the lecture. Take notes on your own paper. Pay attention to Mr. Matos's stress and intonation to help you understand the lecture. ▶ **PLAY**

2 Make sure your notes are in a well-organized format. Then compare them with a partner.

LECTURE, PART TWO: Getting and Keeping a Job

GUESSING VOCABULARY FROM CONTEXT

1 | The following items contain important vocabulary from Part Two of the lecture. Work with a partner. Using the context and your knowledge of related words, take turns trying to guess the meanings of the words in **bold**.

_____ **1** The **procedures** for finding a job and sending an application have changed quite a lot.

_____ **2** You will be expected to complete **multiple** tasks.

_____ **3** If you are looking for any type of **administrative work**, . . .

_____ **4** Forget about the good old days of paper calendars, **rolodexes**, and **file cabinets**.

_____ **5** . . . digital databases that **store** all the information that used to be kept on paper

_____ **6** Many departments use spreadsheet programs to keep track of all **transactions**.

_____ **7** You must have a plan for how to **acquire** these skills.

_____ **8** Even **novice users** can learn how to create professional-looking flyers.

2 | Work with your partner. Match the vocabulary terms with their definitions by writing the letter of each definition below in the blank next to the sentence or phrase containing the correct term in step 1. Check your answers in a dictionary if necessary.

    a beginners
    b managing or organizing documents and information
    c several or many
    d learn, get
    e keep
    f items that hold information on paper
    g buying and selling
    h steps

⌒ NOTE TAKING: USING YOUR NOTES TO ANSWER TEST QUESTIONS

1 | Read the following questions about Part Two of the lecture. Think about what kind of information you will need to answer them.

    1 Why must an applicant be able to participate well in an interview?
    2 Which basic computer skills are expected in an office environment today?
    3 How was information stored in the past? How is it stored today?
    4 What are some ways to acquire or improve the skills you need?

2 | Listen to Part Two of the lecture and take notes on your own paper. Use the questions in step 1 as a guide to help you listen for the important points. ▶ **PLAY**

3 | Use your notes to answer the questions in step 1. Share your answers with a partner. You can take turns explaining your answers orally. Or, you can write your answers and then exchange what you have written. Answer as fully as you can.

AFTER THE LECTURE

SUMMARIZING WHAT YOU HAVE HEARD

Remember that only the most important points of a lecture should be included in a summary.

Write a one-paragraph summary of the lecture. Include these words in your summary:

traditional	computer	research	skills
apply	interview	technology	acquire

APPLYING WHAT YOU HAVE LEARNED

1 Look at this cartoon. Work with a partner and take turns answering the following questions.

  1 Who do you think the woman is talking to?

  2 Do you think the person the woman is talking to will agree with her opinion about what is important?

"Nothing important—nothing on fax, nothing on voice mail, nothing on the Internet. Just, you know, handwritten stuff."

2 Look at this cartoon. Work with your partner and make up the rest of the conversation between the two men in the cartoon. Take turns acting the parts of "Bob" and "the other man."

Bob, I have a terrible confession to make: Not only am I <u>not</u> 'on line', I don't even know what 'on line' means...

SIPRESS

SHARING YOUR OPINION

Answer the questions below in a small group.

  1 What do you think are the three most important qualities in an employee? Why?

  2 What job skills do you think people will need by the year 2050?

Chapter

10

Global Issues

1 GETTING STARTED

In this section you will learn about the worldwide trend toward living in an urban environment, or city. You will begin to think about the advantages and disadvantages of city life.

READING AND THINKING ABOUT THE TOPIC

1 | Read the following passage.

Cities dominate social, economic, and cultural affairs today, but this was not always true. We tend to accept cities as facts of life, but actually they are a relatively recent phenomenon. A century ago, 86% of the world still lived in rural (country) areas, but today about 50% live in rural areas and about 50% live in urban areas (cities). By 2025, it is estimated that over 60% of the population will live in urban areas or suburbs (smaller communities just outside of a city).

City residents are offered a rich life full of excitement and opportunity. All over the world, more and more people are moving to urban environments in search of better jobs, a better education, or the possibility of more lifestyle choices. However, there are also many serious problems in cities, including homelessness, environmental pollution, crime, and noise.

2 | Answer the following questions based on the information in the passage.
   1 How has the population of urban areas changed during the past century?
   2 Why do people move to cities?
   3 What problems have developed in cities?

3 | Read these questions and share your answers with a partner.
   1 What features of city life appeal to you?
   2 What features of city life do you dislike?

EXAMINING GRAPHIC MATERIAL

Look at the graph below and discuss the following questions with a partner.

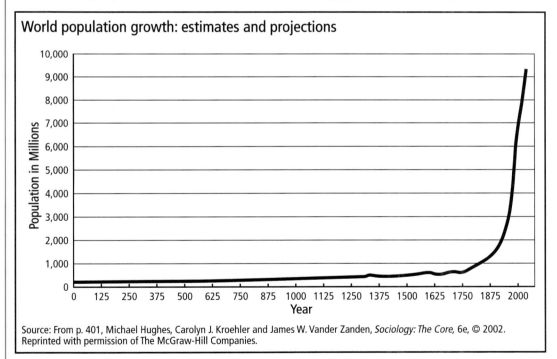

World population growth: estimates and projections

Source: From p. 401, Michael Hughes, Carolyn J. Kroehler and James W. Vander Zanden, *Sociology: The Core*, 6e, © 2002. Reprinted with permission of The McGraw-Hill Companies.

   1 What is the approximate population of the world today?
   2 What can you predict about the population of the world in the year 2050?
   3 In "Reading and Thinking About the Topic," you read that more and more of the world's population is moving to urban areas. What effect do you think that will have on urban life? What effect will it have on rural life?

∩ PERSONALIZING THE TOPIC

Your own experiences can help you to relate to new information that you learn about a topic. Remember that sensory impressions are an important part of experiences.

1 | Think of a city, a suburb, and a place in the country that you know. What sights and sounds do you experience in each of these places? Write down your ideas and share them with a partner.

You are in a city.   Sights: _____

_____

Sounds: _____

_____

You are in a suburb.   Sights: _____

_____

Sounds: _____

_____

You are in the country. Sights: _____

_____

Sounds: _____

_____

2 | Listen to the following sounds. As you listen, fill in the left column of the chart. **▶ PLAY**

What do you think this sound is?	Do you think you would hear this sound in the country, the city, or the suburbs?	How does this sound make you feel?
1 *birds singing*	*country or suburbs*	*peaceful*
2		
3		
4		
5		
6		
7		
8		
9		
10		

3 | Now complete the chart.

4 | Compare your answers to steps 2 and 3 with your partner.

2 AMERICAN VOICES: Barbara and Kenny

In this section you will hear two very different perspectives on quality of life issues. Barbara, a teacher who lives in New York City, discusses urban, suburban, and rural lifestyles. Kenny, an environmental consultant, explains the reasons he has moved from one place to another.

BEFORE THE INTERVIEWS

SHARING YOUR OPINION

1 | Fill in the chart with your opinions about the advantages and disadvantages of life in urban, suburban, and rural environments. Use the box on the right to help you. It shows some of the different factors that affect our quality of life.

	Urban environment	Suburban environment	Rural environment
Advantages		Suburbs are usually safe.	
Disadvantages	Cities can be very dirty.		

Some factors that affect quality of life

Beauty
Cleanliness
Convenience
Education
Employment
Entertainment
Family life
Pace of life
Safety
Transportation

2 | Share your ideas in a small group. Add the ideas of other group members to your chart.

INTERVIEW WITH BARBARA: Life in the city, country, and suburbs

Here are some words and phrases from the interview with Barbara printed in **bold** and given in the context in which you will hear them. They are followed by definitions.

to escape from the urban **ills**: *problems*

unless you like to **putter around** and build things: *spend time doing small projects around the house*

Besides, the country has **bugs**: *insects*

You are being **stung**: *bitten by insects*

People who like a lot of stimulation, you know, can't **hack it**: *are not comfortable with it, dislike it*

The whole car culture thing **kicks in**: *becomes important*

In the country and the suburbs, you're **labeled**: *thought of in a limited, restricted way by your neighbors*

⌒ RETELLING WHAT YOU HAVE HEARD

1 │ Read the following questions before you listen to the interview with Barbara.

    1 What is interesting about living in a city?

    2 What happens when city people go to the country?

    3 Why are cars so important in the country?

    4 What are the pros and cons of the suburbs?

    5 Is city life lonely? Is it dangerous?

Barbara

2 │ Now listen to the interview and take notes. **▶ PLAY**

3 │ Work with a partner. Tell your partner part of the interview, and then let him or her continue. Include answers to the questions in step 1. (You can review your notes first, but do not look at them while you are speaking.)

INTERVIEW WITH KENNY: Pros and cons of city living

Here are some words and phrases from the interview with Kenny printed in **bold** and given in the context in which you will hear them. They are followed by definitions.

What finally **drove me out** was the traffic: *made me leave*

I felt like I was **trapped**: *unable to escape*

I didn't want them **cheering for** different sports teams: *supporting*

I have my ups and downs: *sometimes I feel good and sometimes I feel bad*

My mother was **dropping my daughter off**: *bringing her home*

This is just a **law-abiding** grandmother: *someone who obeys the law*

Other people complain about **graffiti**: *writing on walls*

wild, **remote** places: *distant, away from the city, with few people*

Give me some trees, streams, **boulders**, and animals: *rocks*

on gray **drizzly** days: *rainy*

The gray of the buildings **blends in with** the gray of the sky: *mixes with, becomes like*

the **ideal** place to live: *perfect, best*

🎧 LISTENING FOR DETAILS

1 Read the following questions before you listen to the interview. Make sure you understand the vocabulary. If necessary, use a dictionary to check words that you do not understand.

Kenny

1 Where did Kenny grow up?
- **a** in a small town
- **b** in Europe
- **c** in a city

2 What feeling does being in the country give Kenny?
- **a** isolation
- **b** freedom
- **c** boredom

3 What made Kenny move back to New York from a small town?
- **a** his kids
- **b** his job
- **c** his wife

4 What bothers Kenny most about the urban lifestyle?
- **a** the noise
- **b** the people
- **c** the traffic

5 Which word best describes Kenny's feelings about his mother getting a parking ticket?
- **a** anger
- **b** fear
- **c** stress

6 How does Kenny react to the dirt in the city?
- **a** He really hates it.
- **b** He doesn't mind it.
- **c** He wants to move back to the country.

7 What two places does Kenny like most?
- **a** the suburbs and the country
- **b** the country and the city
- **c** the city and the suburbs

8 When does Kenny dislike the city?
- **a** on rainy days
- **b** on sunny days
- **c** on snowy days

9 What kind of city would Kenny like best?
- **a** a city by the sea
- **b** a city close to a rural area
- **c** a city with beautiful buildings

2 | Now listen to the interview with Kenny. As you listen, circle the correct answer to the questions above. Then compare your answers with a partner. ▶ **PLAY**

AFTER THE INTERVIEWS

DRAWING INFERENCES

1 | Work with a partner. Read the list of activities below. Then, based on what you inferred from the interviews, decide whether you think that Barbara and Kenny would enjoy them. You may decide that only Barbara would like the activity, only Kenny would like it, or that they both would like it. Check (✔) the appropriate boxes.

Activity	Would Probably Like It	
	Barbara	Kenny
1 Having a picnic by a lake	☐	☐
2 Going to the theater	☐	☐
3 Going to a concert in a small, neighborhood park	☐	☐
4 Going camping or hiking in the mountains	☐	☐
5 Going out to a restaurant with friends	☐	☐

2 | Share your answers with the class. Be prepared to support your opinions.

SHARING YOUR OPINION

Look at this cartoon. Discuss the following questions as a class.

1 What do you think the speaker means by "a larger community"?

2 Do you think the cartoonist believes that people who live in cities feel like part of a larger community? Why or why not?

"We love the view. It helps to remind us that we're part of a larger community."

3 IN YOUR OWN VOICE

In this section you will make a questionnaire about factors that affect the quality of life in our living environments. Then you will use your questionnaire in a survey to find out what people think are the ten most important factors and report your findings to the class.

MAKING A QUESTIONNAIRE TO USE IN A SURVEY

Making a clear questionnaire is the first step in conducting a good survey. Most questionnaires ask the interviewees to respond to specific questions so that it is easy to analyze the data that is collected. Many questionnaires also allow room for additional explanations and comments from the interviewees.

1 | Work in a small group. Read the following list of factors that can affect the quality of life in our living environments. Add any other things you can think of to the list.

- Good public transportation
- Bike lanes on streets
- A good climate – not too hot, cold, or wet
- An exciting nightlife with restaurants, cafés, and clubs
- An active cultural life with concert halls, theaters, movies, and museums
- Parks
- Sports facilities, such as pools and tennis courts
- Sports stadiums
- Good schools
- Safe streets patrolled by police officers
- Adequate parking
- Good shopping areas
- Fresh air with little pollution
- Beautiful architecture
- A low cost of living
- Ethnic, racial, and socioeconomic diversity

2 Using the list, work with a partner to make a questionnaire. Your questionnaire should look something like the chart below. Include a row for each factor. Make sure that you leave enough room to take notes on any interesting comments that your interviewees make. Use a separate chart for each interviewee.

Factor	How Important Is This Factor to You?			Comments
	Extremely important	Somewhat important	Not very important	
Good public transportation				
Bike lanes in street				

CONDUCTING A SURVEY

1 Work with the same partner you worked with in "Making a Questionnaire to Use in a Survey." Practice introducing yourself and asking questions about the factors on your questionnaire. Here are some things you can say:

- *Hello. I wonder if you'd answer a few questions for me. I'm doing a survey for my class about what factors make an area a good place to live. Would you mind helping me?*
- *I'm going to read you a list of factors and ask you how important these factors are to you, and why. The first factor is public transportation. How important is a good public transportation system to you? Is it extremely important, somewhat important, or not very important?*
- *(After the interviewee has answered) Could you explain why public transportation is (is not) important to you?*

2 Using the questionnaire you have made, conduct a survey of as many people as possible. With your partner, take turns interviewing the people and taking notes on what they say.

3 Work with your partner to analyze your data. For each factor, count the number of responses in each column. Select the ten factors that your interviewees classed as most important.

4 Report your findings to the class.

4 ACADEMIC LISTENING AND NOTE TAKING: Our Changing Cities

In this section you will hear and take notes on a two-part lecture called *Our Changing Cities*. Professor Bryan Gilroy, a frequent lecturer on sociological topics, will discuss some of the reasons why more and more people are choosing to live in urban areas. Then he will talk about some of the changes that are occurring in our cities.

BEFORE THE LECTURE

BUILDING BACKGROUND KNOWLEDGE ON THE TOPIC

1 │ Work in a small group. Take the following quiz to see how much you know about cities.

   1 Name ten capital cities in the world.

   2 What is the city with the largest population in the United States?

   3 What is the tallest building in the world?

   4 What is the most important official of a city called?

   5 Which city has the oldest subway?

   6 What is the city with the largest population in the world?

2 │ Check your answers at the bottom of page 150.

STUDYING HANDOUTS

> It is common for lecturers to distribute handouts to accompany their lectures. The handouts might include charts or graphs, an outline, or a bibliography or suggested reading list. When you are given a handout before a lecture, study it carefully. Handouts will give you a preview of some of the ideas the lecturer will discuss.

1 │ Work with a partner. Look at Handout 1, on page 150, for Part One of the lecture. It is taken from a book by Ebenezer Howard that was written over one hundred years ago. Because it was written so long ago, some of the vocabulary may seem unfamiliar, but do not be concerned. As you study the handout, you will see many words and concepts that you can understand.

   1 Highlight the ideas or vocabulary that you understand.

   2 Discuss the following questions.

     a Howard calls the places he presents "Town," "Country," and "Town-Country." What places do you think these correspond to today?

     b According to Howard's model, which place seems to have the most advantages? Do you agree?

     c Why do you think Howard chose the image of magnets to illustrate his idea?

HANDOUT 1: Ebenezer Howard's Model

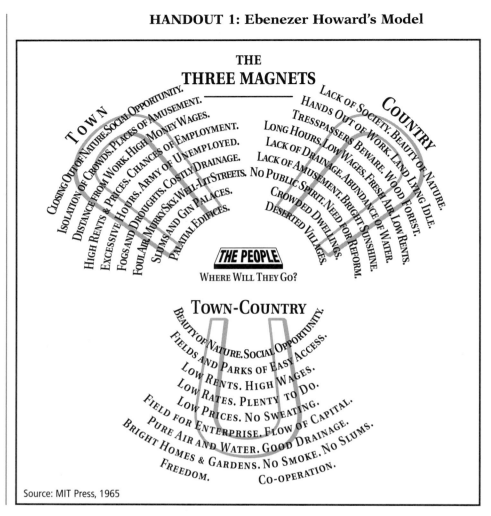

THE
THREE MAGNETS

TOWN

CLOSING OUT OF NATURE. SOCIAL OPPORTUNITY.
ISOLATION OF CROWDS. PLACES OF AMUSEMENT.
DISTANCE FROM WORK. HIGH MONEY WAGES.
HIGH RENTS & PRICES. CHANCES OF EMPLOYMENT.
EXCESSIVE HOURS. ARMY OF UNEMPLOYED.
FOGS AND DROUGHTS. COSTLY DRAINAGE.
FOUL AIR. MURKY SKY. WELL-LIT STREETS.
SLUMS AND GIN PALACES.
PALATIAL EDIFICES.

COUNTRY

LACK OF SOCIETY. BEAUTY OF NATURE.
HANDS OUT OF WORK. LAND LYING IDLE.
TRESSPASSERS BEWARE. WOOD, FOREST.
LONG HOURS. LOW WAGES. FRESH AIR. LOW RENTS.
LACK OF DRAINAGE. ABUNDANCE OF WATER.
LACK OF AMUSEMENT. BRIGHT SUNSHINE.
NO PUBLIC SPIRIT. NEED FOR REFORM.
CROWDED DWELLINGS.
DESERTED VILLAGES.

THE PEOPLE
WHERE WILL THEY GO?

TOWN-COUNTRY

BEAUTY OF NATURE. SOCIAL OPPORTUNITY.
FIELDS AND PARKS OF EASY ACCESS.
LOW RENTS. HIGH WAGES.
LOW RATES. PLENTY TO DO.
LOW PRICES. NO SWEATING.
FIELD FOR ENTERPRISE. FLOW OF CAPITAL.
PURE AIR AND WATER. GOOD DRAINAGE.
BRIGHT HOMES & GARDENS. NO SMOKE. NO SLUMS.
FREEDOM.   CO-OPERATION.

Source: MIT Press, 1965

2 Look at Handout 2, on page 151, from Part Two of the lecture. During the past century, different models have been drawn to show the way that cities grow and spread. The three models in this handout are among the best known.

1 Work with your partner. Find out the meaning of any vocabulary that you don't know. You can ask other classmates, use a dictionary, or ask your teacher for help.

2 Discuss the following questions.

   a How would you describe the differences between the three models?

   b Do you know any cities that look similar to any of these three models?

HANDOUT 2: Patterns of Urban Development

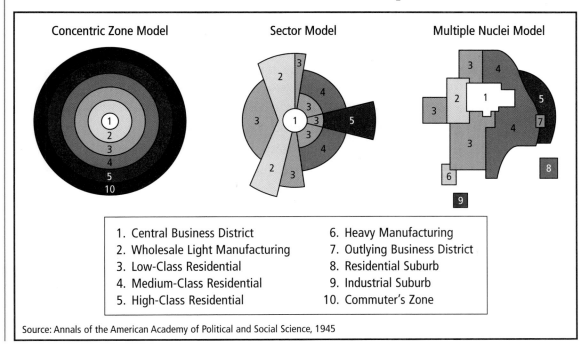

Concentric Zone Model   Sector Model   Multiple Nuclei Model

1. Central Business District
2. Wholesale Light Manufacturing
3. Low-Class Residential
4. Medium-Class Residential
5. High-Class Residential
6. Heavy Manufacturing
7. Outlying Business District
8. Residential Suburb
9. Industrial Suburb
10. Commuter's Zone

Source: Annals of the American Academy of Political and Social Science, 1945

🎧 NOTE TAKING: USING HANDOUTS TO HELP YOU TAKE NOTES

A lecturer's handouts will help you understand the lecture and give you material that you can study later. However, lecturers rarely give you exactly the same information in the lecture as they do in handouts. Therefore, you must still listen carefully to understand what the speaker says.

Here are some ways that you can take notes on handouts as you listen to a lecture:

- highlight or circle parts of the handout that the lecturer discusses
- mark information that you do not understand and want to ask questions about
- write comments

Remember to take notes in your usual way in addition to marking the handouts. Be sure to organize all your notes in a clear format (*e.g.*, columns, an outline, or a map) after the lecture.

1 | Listen to two excerpts from the lecture, one from Part One and one from Part Two. Circle the parts of the handouts that the lecturer refers to. Take notes on your own paper about what he says. ▶ **PLAY**

2 | Compare your notes with a partner.

LECTURE, PART ONE: Reasons People Move to Cities

GUESSING VOCABULARY FROM CONTEXT

1 | The following items contain some important vocabulary from Part One of the lecture. Work with a partner. Using the context and your knowledge of related words, take turns trying to guess the meanings of the words in **bold**.

_____ **1** we are going to discuss the mass **urbanization** of the world's population.

_____ **2** . . . which is an **unprecedented** trend worldwide.

_____ **3** The town has "social opportunity" but "**isolation**."

_____ **4** Until the twentieth century, the major source of employment was **farming**.

_____ **5** Jobs are being created in **manufacturing.**

_____ **6** Jobs are being created in **financing**.

_____ **7** There are transportation **networks**.

2 | Work with your partner. Match the vocabulary terms with their definitions by writing the letter of each definition below in the blank next to the sentence or phrase containing the correct term in step 1. Check your answers in a dictionary if necessary.

  a raising animals or growing fruits and vegetables to sell
  b making products in factories
  c movement to the cities
  d something that has never happened before
  e systems of roads, buses, and trains that cross and connect with each other
  f separation from other people; loneliness
  g management of money

🎧 NOTE TAKING: COMBINING THE SKILLS

In this book, you have learned many skills that can help you to take clear notes on lectures.

As you listen to a lecture, you have learned how to:
- identify main ideas and supporting details
- identify numerical information
- identify organizational phrases and signal words
- pay attention to the lecturer's stress and intonation

As you take notes, you have learned how to:
- use symbols and abbreviations
- use telegraphic language
- record numerical information accurately
- use handouts
- organize your notes in an appropriate format, _e.g.,_ columns, map, outline
- write questions and comments about what you have heard

After you listen to a lecture, you have learned how to:
- clarify anything you have not understood
- revise and organize your notes clearly, if necessary

As you continue to practice, you will find that you can easily combine all these note-taking skills whenever you take notes.

1 | Listen to Part One of the lecture and take notes. Practice combining the skills that you have learned. ▶ PLAY

2 | Revise your notes and organize them more clearly if necessary. How satisfied are you with your note-taking progress? Are there any areas that you need to review?

3 | Compare your notes with a partner and share your questions and comments.

LECTURE, PART TWO: Changes in the City

GUESSING VOCABULARY FROM CONTEXT

1 | The following items contain some important vocabulary from Part One of the lecture. Work with a partner. Using the context and your knowledge of related words, take turns trying to guess the meanings of the words in **bold**.

_____ **1** Tokyo, Mexico, Bombay, and São Paulo are just a few examples of today's **megacities**.

_____ **2** They show the **urban sprawl** that is occurring in contemporary cities.

_____ **3** Our cities are breaking up into smaller communities, often by ethnic group or **income level**.

_____ **4** Many cities do have a kind of identity or personality, but a city is not **homogeneous**.

_____ **5** Many cities have slum areas or ghettos where people live in **destitute** conditions.

_____ **6** The beautiful architecture and **vibrant** nightlife are one face of the city.

2 | Work with your partner. Match the vocabulary terms with their definitions by writing the letter of each definition below in the blank next to the correct term in step 1. Check your answers in a dictionary if necessary.

a exciting
b uncontrolled growth of cities
c all the same
d very poor and hopeless
e the amount of money that people make
f huge cities

NOTE TAKING: COMBINING THE SKILLS

1 | Listen to Part Two of the lecture and take notes on your own paper. **▶ PLAY**

2 | Revise and reorganize your notes if necessary.

3 | Exchange your notes with a partner. Use the checklist below to evaluate your partner's notes. Check (✔) the skills that your partner used.

Note-taking Skills
☐ Identifying main ideas and supporting details
☐ Recording numerical information
☐ Using symbols and abbreviations
☐ Using telegraphic language
☐ Organizing notes clearly in columns, a map, or an outline
☐ Using the lecturer's handouts
☐ Identifying anything that was not clear
☐ Writing questions and comments

4 | Work with your partner and review each other's note-taking skills.

5 | Discuss your questions and comments with your partner. Clarify anything you still do not understand by asking other classmates.

AFTER THE LECTURE

SUMMARIZING WHAT YOU HAVE HEARD

1 | Look at the first part of a summary of the lecture. Use your notes to finish writing the summary.

> Our Changing Cities
> Professor Bryan Gilroy
>
> Many more people are moving to cities today than in the past. There are various reasons for this, some of which are shown in the handout from Ebenezer Howard's book. The main reason that many people prefer to live in a city is because there are more jobs and more opportunities to earn money in urban environments. A second reason is that cities offer comfort and convenience. . . .

2 | Compare your summary with a partner. Remember that your summaries will not be exactly the same.

GIVING GROUP PRESENTATIONS

Remember that when you give group presentations, it is important for every member of a group to make an equal contribution. Review the guidelines for giving group presentations on page 73.

1 | Professor Gilroy mentioned that many cities have their own "identity" or "personality." Look at the following pictures. Do you recognize these cities? What helped you to identify them?

2 | Work in a small group. Choose a city that you know well or a city that you would like to visit. Do not choose the same city as other groups.

NAME OF CITY: _____

3 | Work with your group. Use the categories below to help you describe the identity and personality of the city you have chosen. Add other categories of your own. You may want to do research in a library or on the Internet. If possible, use photographs to illustrate what you want to say.

CATEGORIES: geographic location
size of city
weather
cultural activities
typical food
customs or traditions
architecture
transportation
problems facing city

4 | Practice your presentation and then give it in front of the class.

CREDITS

Text Credits

16 From p. 102, Introduction to Sociology (with Info Trac) 7th edition by TISCHLER. © 2002. Reprinted with permission of Wadsworth, a division of Thomson Learning: www.thomsonrights.com. Fax 800 730-2215.

22 U.S. Dept. of Health and Human Services, National Institute on Drug Abuse, *Monitoring the Future Study*, 1999.

40 The original study was *Gendered heteronormativity*, conducted by Joyce McCarl Nielsen, Glenda Walden and Charlotte A. Kunkel. The Sociological Quarterly, 41(2), 2000.

50 U.S. Department of Labor, Bureau of Labor Statistics, *Employment and Earnings*, 2000.

57 From p. 258, Michael Hughes, Carolyn J. Kroehler and James W. Vander Zanden, *Sociology: The Core*, 6e, © 2002. Reprinted with permission of The McGraw-Hill Companies.

58 From *Paths to Power: A Woman's Guide from First Job to Executive*, by Natasha Josefowitz, 1990. Used with permission of the author.

83 From p. 392, Introduction to Sociology, 3e, Anthony Giddens and Mitchell Duneier, Norton, 2000

89 The original study was *The Un-TV Experiment*, conducted by Bernard McGrane. Teaching Sociology, 21, 1993.

91 From *The New York Times 2002 Almanac*

95 Quoted in *The Economist*, June 9, 1990, p.6.

101 U.S. Department of Justice, Bureau of Justice Statistics, Washington, DC: U.S. Government Printing Office

104 From p. 170, Introduction to Sociology (with Info Trac) 7th edition by TISCHLER. © 2002. Reprinted with permission of Wadsworth, a division of Thomson Learning: www.thomsonrights.com. Fax 800 730-2215.

119 From p. 163, Michael Hughes, Carolyn J. Kroehler and James W. Vander Zanden, *Sociology: The Core*, 6e, © 2002. Reprinted with permission of The McGraw-Hill Companies.

121 From p. 185, Introduction to Sociology (with Info Trac) 7th edition by TISCHLER. © 2002. Reprinted with permission of Wadsworth, a division of Thomson Learning: www.thomsonrights.com. Fax 800 730-2215.

126 Based on a 1995 Hart Research Poll of police chiefs in the United States. Death Penalty Information Center. Used by permission.

130 "Technology" by Angeline A. Moscatt. Used with permission of the author.

133 From p. 445, Michael Hughes, Carolyn J. Kroehler and James W. Vander Zanden, *Sociology: The Core*, 6e, © 2002. Reprinted with permission of The McGraw-Hill Companies.

141 From p. 401, Michael Hughes, Carolyn J. Kroehler and James W. Vander Zanden, *Sociology: The Core*, 6e, © 2002. Reprinted with permission of The McGraw-Hill Companies.

150 From Ebenezer Howard, Garden Cities of Tomorrow, MIT Press, Cambridge, Mass., 1965.

151 From "The Nature of Cities," Annals of the American Academy of Political and Social Science, vol. 242, 1945.

Photographic credits

1   © Picture Quest

2   *(left)* © Corbis; *(right)* © Creatas

9   © Corbis

17   © Corbis

31   *(left)* © Getty Images; *(right)* © Michael Keller/Corbis

32   © Corbis

39   *(clockwise from top left)* © Corbis; © Jennie Woodcock; Reflections Photolibrary/Corbis; © Ted Spiegel/Corbis; © Jose Luis Pelaez, Inc./Corbis

49   *(left)* © Rolf Bruderer/Corbis; *(right)* © Ariel Skelley/Corbis

65   *(clockwise from left)* © Getty Images; © Corbis; © Picture Quest; © Getty Images; © Hemera; © Thinkstock

66   © Getty Images

81   © George Disario/Corbis

97   © William Whitehurst/Corbis

98   © Getty Images

99   © Getty Images

113 © Getty Images

127 © Getty Images

128 © Getty Images

140 © Alan Schein Photography/Corbis

157 *(left to right)* © Getty Images; © Getty Images; © Corbis

Illustration credits

JT Morrow: 34

Dominic Bugatto: 42, 52, 105, 147

Mick Stevens: 64

Robert Weber: 72, 146

Sidney Harris: 112

Warren Miller: 139 *(top)*

David Sipress: 139 *(bottom)*

TASK INDEX

Page numbers in boldface indicate tasks that are headed by commentary boxes.